Contents

At **Little Worship Company**, our heart is to inspire and delight young children with a knowledge of God and to support them as they begin to take their first steps of faith. Our range of beautifully-crafted, Biblically-based resources have been designed to equip families and churches as they help children to discover more of the God who made them and loves them completely.

The Bible Curriculum

SERIES 1

For associated media head over to

With thanks to Lee Bruce, Tim Dobson, Sarah Joy, Colse Leung, Rachel Noyce, Jo Sunderland and Jenny Sykes.

ISBN: 978-1-9160820-5-2

Introduction

1 ABOUT THE LITTLE WORSHIP COMPANY CURRICULUM GUIDE

This pack comprises four distinct curriculums: **Amazing Me, Beautiful World, Praise Party** and **Wonderful Day.** Each curriculum includes eight flexible session outlines, a template for all-age worship and additional worksheets and resources. These curriculums help young children to explore the building blocks of the Christian faith: who God is, who they are, and the dynamic relationship that God invites them into with Him.

AMAZING ME

We are all God's children, made and loved by our Heavenly Father. In **Amazing Me,** children will explore how special they are – discovering not only the amazing people they were made to be, but the even *more* amazing God who invites them to be His friends.

BEAUTIFUL WORLD

Our world is amazing! **Beautiful World** takes children on a journey through the creation story, inspiring wonder in the incredible world they live in and helping them to see the God who made, knows and loves it – and who made, knows and loves them too.

PRAISE PARTY

Everyone loves a party – and the best ones of all are praise parties! **Praise Party** helps children to understand what it means to praise and worship God, not only with singing, dancing and instruments, but with their hearts, feet and hands too.

WONDERFUL DAY

The Bible is full of God's good promises to us. **Wonderful Day** helps children to explore what these mean for them today, from the moment they wake up until they go to bed, and what it means for them to love and live for God each day in turn.

Throughout this book and our DVDs you'll spot our LOVE BUGS. They might be little – but they remind us of God's BIG love for us.

HOW TO USE THIS RESOURCE

Each session plan is based around a core **Little Big Idea** (learning aim) and can be used flexibly within a range of discipleship and outreach contexts.

The session plan comprises the following elements:

ICE-BREAKER

This is a light-hearted game or challenge, lasting around five minutes, linked to the overall theme of the session. (These are generally pitched at children at the older end of the age range.)

LITTLE BIG QUESTION

This is a simple question that more directly introduces children to the session's theme.

LITTLE BIG IDEA

This element provides the core learning for the session. It is broken up into the following sections:

- **Illustration:** an engaging means of introducing children to the key learning concept explored in the message. This should last around five minutes.
- **Message:** a template for how you might choose to explain the key learning concept, which can be adapted for your unique context and audience. This should take no more than two minutes.

LET'S WORSHIP

This element contains a couple of song suggestions and a simple prayer, all of which are found on the curriculum DVD. (Note: the songs can be played with subtitles so that the children can join in.)

- **Song:** A contemporary worship song or hymn played over a beautiful filmed sequence.
- **Singalong:** A simple song drawing on key curriculum themes, which children could easily learn and join in with over the course of several weeks.
- **All-age liturgy:** A simple prayer of thanksgiving based on the curriculum theme, which the children could learn over the course of the series.

LITTLE GROUPS

This element contains a suggested activity that allows children to respond to or further explore key concepts outlined in the Little Big Idea – for example, through creative prayer, small group discussion or practical action. These last around ten minutes.

SESSION PRAYER

This is a simple prayer response based on the session's theme.

GET CRAFTY!

Each session contains three suggested craft activities which serve as a reminder of the session's key learning. Some of these crafts can also be found on the DVD. These are marked with this symbol: [DVD] These can be used either within the session to guide the children as they make the craft, or to help you prepare for the session in advance.

There are also colouring sheets containing the relevant Bible verse available to photocopy. These are included at the end of each session.

In the following pages we have included some suggestions for how you might combine the different elements in a range of church-based contexts. It is worth noting, however, that each group of children is different, and that you are best placed to decide what would work well in your unique setting.

You will find a number of **symbols** throughout the session outlines.

Preparation level: An at-a-glance indication of the amount of preparation required for that particular element. There are three levels.

- *zero* No preparation at all
- *easy* A small amount of preparation required
- *medium* Slightly more committed preparation required

Craft difficulty level: These indicate whether the activity is accessible to children of all ages or geared towards older children.

- *suitable for all ages*
- *for older children*

Which curriculum elements you use will depend on where you want to use this resource, and the age of the children you work with. Below are some suggestions which may be helpful.

OUTREACH	SUNDAY SCHOOL		ALL-AGE WORSHIP	
TODDLER GROUP	AGES 0-4	AGES 5-7	SUNDAY	MESSY CHURCH EXTRA
THE BIG IDEA: TALK ONLY	THE BIG IDEA: ILLUSTRATION & TALK	ICE-BREAKER	THE BIG IDEA: ILLUSTRATION & TALK	THE BIG IDEA: ILLUSTRATION & TALK
LET'S WORSHIP	LET'S WORSHIP	THE BIG IDEA: ILLUSTRATION & TALK	LET'S WORSHIP	LET'S WORSHIP
GET CRAFTY: YOUNGER CHILDREN	GET CRAFTY: YOUNGER CHILDREN	LET'S WORSHIP	GET CRAFTY	GET CRAFTY
		LITTLE GROUPS		
		GET CRAFTY: OLDER CHILDREN		

USING LITTLE WORSHIP COMPANY RESOURCES IN SUNDAY SCHOOL

Little Worship Company resources can be used to help young disciples explore God and His wonderful promises to them within the context of Sunday children's church.

The session templates below are aimed at two distinct age groups: preschool (0-4) and school age (5-7). If your groups do not fit easily into these categories, please read through the entire session plan and select and/or adapt the elements as you see fit for your unique context.

Sunday School discipleship: 0-4 years

SESSION AIM

The aim of this session is to nurture young children in their growing faith.

Taking place within a wider context of Sunday worship, the session allows space and opportunity to introduce key Christian beliefs about God and His promises in an age-appropriate way.

PREPARING THE SPACE

Set up age-appropriate toys at different play stations. Select a simple **craft** (or at most two). Have it prepped and ready at a craft table. Provide copies of the session's **colouring sheet.**

Prepare a snack for the children to share.

Session plan (based on a 1-hour session)

Free play: 20 minutes

- Allow the children a choice of free play/art and craft.

Introduction and snack time: 10 minutes

- Sit the children at a table and give them a small snack and drink.
- Play the session's **worship song** as the children eat, to introduce the session theme.
- Depending on the children's ages, you may also like to ask them the **Little Big Question.**

Little Big Idea: 7 minutes

- Sit together on the floor.
- Run the **illustration.**
- Share the **message.**

Worship: 3 minutes

- Sing the **singalong** together.
- Say the **all-age liturgy** together and/or close with the **session prayer.**

Free play: 20 minutes

- Allow the children a choice of free play/art and craft.

Sunday School discipleship: 5-7 years

SESSION AIM

The aim of this session is to support slightly older children in their developing faith. Taking place within a wider context of Sunday worship, the session allows adequate space and opportunity to explore and then reflect on key Christian beliefs in an age-appropriate way.

PREPARING THE SPACE

Select one or two suggested **crafts.** Have them prepped and ready at a craft table. Provide copies of the session's **colouring sheet**.

You may like to have the **Little Big Question** displayed on a board as the children enter, along with pens, paper and a questions box.

Prepare a few age-appropriate play activities for the end of the session and a snack for the children to share.

Session plan (based on a 1-hour session)

Welcome and snack time: 10 minutes

Sit the children in groups and give them a snack and a drink. Invite them to answer the **Little Big Question.** (You may like to give them pens and paper to write their answer down and put in the box at the front to be read out later.)

Introduction: 5-10 minutes

Lead the children in the **session game or challenge.**

Little Big Idea: 7 minutes

- Sit together on the floor.
- Run the **illustration.**
- Share the **message.** You may like to incorporate the children's responses to the session's **Little Big Question** here.

Worship: up to 5 minutes

- Sing the session worship song and/or the **singalong.**
- You might like to say the **all-age liturgy** together.

Explore more: 10 minutes

- Break the children into smaller groups and lead them in the suggested **discussion or response.**
- Close with the **session prayer.**

Free play: 20 minutes

- Allow the children a choice of free play/art and craft.

3 USING LITTLE WORSHIP COMPANY RESOURCES AT TODDLER GROUPS

The weekly toddler group provides many children with their first, and sometimes only, experience of church. **Little Worship Company** resources can be used in this context to introduce children and their families – who may have no prior knowledge of the Christian faith – to some of its core beliefs.

The template below incorporates worship, a short message and a prayer within a stay-and-play session. If your group is unused to any particularly Christian content in the current format, you might want to consider introducing these elements gradually and explaining the changes to parents and carers.

Start by spending a few weeks using **crafts** and **Bible colouring sheets** on a particular theme, sharing its significance at the craft table. For example, on Week 1 put play dough out alongside the Psalm 139:14 colouring sheet (**Amazing Me** session 1). As you explain the craft, share how the Bible teaches that we are all wonderfully made by God.

Next, pick a **singalong song** to learn within song time. Again, ensure that you explain what the song means and why you are singing it. Don't forget to include fun actions!

You might then choose to show **the whole DVD** as a special event at the end of a term. Put out beanbags, comfy chairs, popcorn and drinks (as if at the cinema) or provide instruments and invite the children to play along.

SESSION AIM

This context is best understood as outreach rather than discipleship: a means of gently and respectfully introducing people to the Christian faith within the wider context of a warm and welcoming community. As such, we have suggested a 'lighter' version of the **0-4 Sunday School** programme – a simple song, brief 'thought' and prayer – to sit alongside the usual play, art and craft, snack and story times.

PREPARING THE SPACE

Set up age-appropriate toys at different play stations. Select a simple **craft** (or at most two). Have it prepped and ready at a craft table. Provide copies of the session's **colouring sheet.**

Prepare a snack for the children to share.

Session outline (based on a 1½-hour stay-and-play session)

Free play: 1 hour

- Allow the children a choice of free play/art and craft.

Snack time: 10 minutes

- Sit the children at a table and give them a small snack and drink.
- Play the session's worship song as the children eat, to introduce the session theme.

Reflection: 5 minutes

- Share a simple thought, based on the session's **message.** Remember to make the link between the craft and the message.
- Sing the session **singalong.** (Use actions as much as possible!)
- Close with the **session prayer.**

Songs and games: 15 minutes

Following the reflection, you might like to include some more conventional children's songs, stories or simple games to close the session.

USING LITTLE WORSHIP COMPANY RESOURCES IN ALL-AGE WORSHIP

All-age worship provides a fantastic opportunity for all God's children, young and old, to praise and worship God together – whether that's in the context of a regular Sunday service or in a less formal 'café church' setting.

The combined **Little Worship Company** resources provide a bank of material that can be used flexibly within these contexts to create a meaningful and inclusive worship service for the whole church family.

Each DVD contains:

- **Eight hymns and worship songs** which will be familiar to diverse age groups. These can be played with subtitled lyrics for use in worship.
- Additional child-friendly **singalong songs**
- A simple **'thank you' prayer** on the curriculum's theme

As well as the session plans, this church resource book contains additional material specifically for use in all-age worship:

- Suggestions for **Bible readings** which resonate with the curriculum theme
- **All-age prayers** – including family-friendly liturgy and ideas for creative prayer responses

These can be found in the appendix to each curriculum.

We have created two sample service plans for all-age worship (below): one for a 'traditional' Sunday service; one for a less formal outreach service.

'Sunday' all-age worship

At the end of the curriculum, you may like to lead a Sunday all-age worship service on the curriculum's theme, inviting the children to participate in leading it. There is a suggested service plan in the Bible Curriculum for **Amazing Me, Beautiful World, Praise Party** and **Wonderful Day,** which you can follow or adapt it as appropriate for your congregation.

Intergenerational café church (Messy Church Extra)

Many churches today run all-age worship services with a clear outreach focus. These tend to be less formal than the traditional 'Sunday morning' service, with significant time given to craft activities and eating together alongside the more conventional elements of worship (i.e. singing, Bible reading and prayer). These services may take place at other points in the weekend or after school during the week in order to appeal to families who are unused or unable to attend church on a Sunday.

Below you will find our suggestions for using **Little Worship Company** resources in this context. Unlike the 'Sunday service' template – which incorporates elements from the DVD and additional worship resources to compliment prior use of the curriculum in Sunday School – this service template draws on the **individual curriculum session plans**, allowing for several all-age worship events per curriculum. We would recommend that you browse the session plans for each curriculum, selecting 3 or 4 to run as a mini-curriculum across the term.

PREPARING THE SPACE

Set up different craft stations around your venue. Use the **crafts** suggested in that session's **Get Crafty!** section.

Set up an area of the room for your 'core' worship elements – whether chairs at café-style tables, or a theatre-style seating area.

Service plan (based on a 1¼-hour plan)

Craft activities: 25 minutes

Welcome the congregation as they arrive. Introduce the theme of the service and invite them to participate in the different craft activities.

After about 25 minutes, invite the congregation to move to a separate area of the room for the core 'worship' elements.

Introduction: 3 minutes

Welcome your congregation and explain today's theme. You might like to ask a few people the **Little Big Question.**

Worship: 8 minutes

Lead the congregation in **sung worship** using one or two worship songs from the DVD. (Turn the subtitles to 'on' so that people can sing along.)

Little Big Idea: 7 minutes

- Run the **illustration.**
- Share the **message.**

Worship: 7 minutes

Sing one of the recommended **singalong songs** and/or select another worship song.

- Pray together. Choose one from the curriculum appendix, the curriculum **all-age liturgy** or use the **session prayer.**

Eat together: 25 minutes

Continue in fellowship and conversation over food.

Amazing Me Bible curriculum

AMAZING ME

We are all God's children, made and loved by our Heavenly Father. In **Amazing Me**, the children will explore how special they are – discovering not only the amazing people they were made to be, but the even MORE amazing God who invites them to be His friends.

1 GOD MADE ME

In this session, the children will:

- explore what makes them unique
- understand that they have been made by God and are known by Him

You created every single tiny bit of me. You put me together in my mummy's tummy. THANK YOU, GOD. I am brilliantly and marvellously made. Psalm 139:13-14 (LWC)

2 GOD LOVES ME

In this session, the children will:

- explore what it means to be a beloved child
- understand that they are God's precious children and what it means to have a Father in Heaven

I am God's very special treasure. 1 Peter 2:9 (LWC)

3 GOD IS WITH ME AS I GROW

In this session, the children will:

- explore the idea that they will grow and change as they get older
- understand that God will never change and will always love and be with them

Jesus Christ is the same yesterday and today and forever. Hebrews 13:8

4 GOD ASKS ME TO BE HIS FRIEND

In this session, the children will:

- explore the story of God calling Samuel
- understand that we are never too young to know and follow God

Don't let anyone put you down because you're young. 1 Timothy 4:12 (MSG)

5 GOD MADE ME FOR AN ADVENTURE WITH HIM

In this session, the children will:

- explore the idea of being made for a purpose
- understand that God calls us to follow Him and that we can discover what this means by reading the Bible

We are God's best artwork! Ephesians 2:10 (LWC)

6 GOD'S LOVE FOR ME NEVER RUNS OUT

In this session, the children will:

- explore the story of the Lost Sheep
- understand that we are and always will be precious to God; and that God will always forgive us when we make mistakes

He will take great delight in you... He will rejoice over you with singing. Zephaniah 3:17

7 GOD MAKES ME BRAVE

In this session, the children will:

- explore the story of Joshua crossing the Jordan
- understand that God is always with us and that He will give us His courage

Be strong and be courageous. Do not be afraid or troubled, for the Lord your God is with you wherever you go. Joshua 1:9 (LWC)

8 GOD MAKES ME STRONG

In this session, the children will:

- explore the concept of 'strength'
- understand that God is with us and loves us and gives us His strength

I can do anything – Jesus has made me strong! Philippians 4:13 (LWC)

WORSHIP SONGS

The following worship songs appear in the **Amazing Me** DVD.

1 *Mother's Prayer*
2 *Sparkling Eyes*
3 *Bubble of Praise*
4 *Be With You*
5 *Be Thou My Vision*
6 *You're Beautiful*
7 *Oceans*
8 *This is Living*

SINGALONG SONGS

In addition to these worship songs, there are three fantastic, simple singalong songs for you to learn with your children across the eight weeks.

1 *Every Little Hair*
2 *Be Brave and Courageous*
3 *Even Though I'm Teeny Weeny* (found in session 4)

MEMORY VERSE

Each session has a Bible verse attached, which the children might like to learn each week. These have been written into the photocopiable colouring sheets at the end of each session plan.

Younger children, however, might like to learn just one simple verse across the series. We would suggest this verse from Psalm 139:

THANK YOU, GOD. I am brilliantly and marvellously made.

Psalm 139:14 (LWC)

1 God made me

In this session, the children will:

- explore what makes them unique
- understand that they have been made by God and are known by Him

Psalm 139:13-14 (LWC)

You created every single tiny bit of me. You put me together in my mummy's tummy. Thank you, God. I am brilliantly and marvellously made.

Preparation level
zero easy medium

ICE-BREAKER

GAME: SORT IT OUT! 

Play this as one big group or compete against each other in smaller groups. Ask the children to arrange themselves in order of:

- height
- birthday (January – December)
- shoe size

With older children, you might make it a little more challenging. Try ordering by age, or hair length!

LITTLE BIG QUESTION

If you could pick one word to describe yourself, what would it be?

LITTLE BIG IDEA

ILLUSTRATION: THE WORLD'S WORST GAME OF SNAP

Preparation: You'll need a set of cards with which to play snap. Make sure that none of them are the same!

Explain that you are going to play 'snap'.

With younger children, choose large cards – big enough for everybody to see. Play the game as 'you against everybody'. Turn over a card at a time, sticking it to a board or wall so that the children can see each card. Ask them to call 'snap' when you reveal a card that is the same as one already on display.

With older children, use a regular deck of cards. Invite a volunteer to help. Split the deck in two. Keep one half and give the other to your volunteer. Call "1, 2, 3, draw!" On draw, each of you takes your top card and displays it to the rest of the children. Explain that they must call 'snap' if the cards are the same. (Which they won't ever be!)

LINK TO MESSAGE

After several rounds, explain that it isn't actually possible to play snap with these cards. They are all one of a kind – unique. No two are the same. And the same is true of us.

You might like to show the **session Bible verse**, found on the DVD, here. 

MESSAGE

- Take a look around at the other children beside you. Every one of us is different.
- We are different on the outside. We come in different sizes. We might have different eye, hair or skin colour.
- We're also different on the inside. We are all good at doing different things. We have different personalities. In other words, the way we feel, think and act are different.
- The word for this is 'unique'. It means, one of a kind. There's nobody else in the world quite like you (or you, or you).
- The Bible says that God made each one of us special. Psalm 139:13-14 says, "You [God] created every single tiny bit of me. You put me together in my mummy's tummy. Thank you, God. I am brilliantly and marvellously made." It's a picture of God putting us together, a bit like an artist carefully making an amazing piece of art.
- It's wonderful to think that God knows everything about us. The colour of our eyes and our hair, the things we're good at, even the things that make us laugh and cry – He made, knows and *loves* it all.

LET'S WORSHIP

Song: *Mother's Prayer*

Singalong: *Every Little Hair*

Prayer: Amazing Me thank you prayer

LITTLE GROUPS

GOD'S WORK OF ART 

You will need: *psalm picture frame worksheet (found in the appendix), pens and pencils or crayons*

Give each child a copy of the picture frame worksheet. Invite them to draw a picture of themselves inside.

Encourage them to draw themselves doing what they love best, or with the people or things they love best, so that it expresses the things that make them uniquely 'them'.

At the end, create an art gallery. Thank God for His amazing works of art.

SESSION PRAYER

Dear God, thank you that we are all made and loved by You. Thank you that You know every single part of us and that we are incredibly special to You. **Amen.**

GET CRAFTY!

Difficulty level

Each of us is made by God and special to Him. Use these crafts to help children reflect on how He made and knows them.

1 LIFE-SIZE DRAWING

You will need: *rolls of brown paper, pens, scissors, decorating materials*

Roll the brown paper out on the floor. Draw around the child as they lie on the paper. Let the child decorate the picture.

2 3D MODEL

You will need: *a range of craft items from your house or garden, sticky tape or glue, materials to decorate*

Preparation: Collect items for modelling, e.g. junk modelling materials, paper plates, pine cones, sticks, shells, etc.

Put the modelling materials onto the floor or craft table. Invite the children to make a face or a person out of the items.

You might want to do this in groups, to make a larger-than-life person on the floor. Bring in some clothes or shoes to help make the body shape.

3 DVD MOULDING CLAY PEOPLE

You will need: *play dough or modelling clay, garlic press, googly eyes*

Preparation: Make some play dough. *[Follow our recipe, found in the appendix.]*

To make play-dough people:

- Make balls of different sizes out of play dough to represent the head and body, and sausage shapes for limbs.
- Put them together, smoothing them out to make a standing body.
- Add details to the face: googly eyes, ears, nose and mouth.
- Run some play dough through the garlic press to make hair and add it to the play-dough person.

To make this simpler for younger children, provide a gingerbread man cutter to make a 2D person.

As you make your play-dough people, talk about how God made them and loves them.

I am
brilliantly
and
marvellously
made
Psalm
139:14
LWC
Little
WORSHIP
Company
AM1

2 God loves me

In this session, the children will:

- explore what it means to be a beloved child
- understand that they are God's precious children, and what it means to have a Father in Heaven

1 Peter 2:9 (LWC)

I am God's very special treasure.

ICE-BREAKER

Preparation level
zero easy medium

TREASURE HUNT! 

You will need: *chocolate coins*

Preparation: Hide your 'treasure' – i.e. the chocolate coins – around the room before the children come in.

Explain to the children that there is treasure hidden all over the room. Can they find it?

Tip: To make sure that everybody has a fair amount of 'treasure', ask the children to put the coins back in the 'treasure chest' (i.e. a box or bucket by you!) when they find them. Then you can share them out equally at a convenient time.

LITTLE BIG QUESTION

Who are your favourite people and why?

LITTLE BIG IDEA

ILLUSTRATION: PRECIOUS CHILD 

Preparation: Invite somebody with a baby/young infant to join you for this part of the session. Ask them to bring the baby so that the children can connect the image of the parent holding a child with the idea of God holding them.

Introduce your guests (parent and baby). Explain that they are here to talk about their precious child.

You might like to ask the following questions:

- What are your baby's favourite things? What do they do that make you smile?
- How did you feel when you first saw your baby?
- What kinds of things do you do every day to look after your baby?

Invite the children to ask questions too.

If your guest is happy with this, you might like to invite the children to play with or cuddle the baby.

Tip: Alternatively, you could invite a parent to talk about their experience of becoming/being a parent, showing pictures of themselves with their child as a baby.

LINK TO MESSAGE

Explain that this child is really precious to their mummy/daddy. The Bible says that we are precious to God in the same way.

You might like to show the **session Bible verse**, found on the DVD, here. 

MESSAGE

- What are the favourite things you have? Who are the people who are most special to you? Think about how it feels to be with them.
- This might give us a bit of an idea about how God feels about us!
- We have seen how God made us – His amazing work of art. But we are not *just* God's special *creation*. The Bible says that we are His special *children* too.
- The Bible says that God made us, He knows us, and He really, really loves us. In fact, 1 Peter 2:9 says that we are "God's very special treasure". That's a way of saying that we are really precious to God.
- The Bible says that God is our amazing Heavenly Dad. He loves us even more than the very best mummy or daddy on Earth loves their child.
- The Bible promises that God is always with us. He carries us when we get tired. He hugs us when we feel sad. And there's nothing in the world that can ever stop Him from loving us.

LET'S WORSHIP

Song: *Sparkling Eyes*

Singalong: *Every Little Hair*

Prayer: Amazing Me thank you prayer

LITTLE GROUPS

IN GOD'S FAMILY

You will need: *small card 'people', pens and colouring pencils, big sheet of paper, sticky tack*

Preparation: Draw a 'family tree' on the paper and display it on a wall.

Give each child a little card 'person' shape. Ask them to decorate it as themselves and to write their name on it.

Invite the children to add themselves to God's family tree. Pray together, thanking God that we are all His precious children.

SESSION PRAYER

Dear God, thank you that every one of us is Your special treasure and that You are our Big Heavenly Dad. Thank you that You are with us and that You love us more than we will ever know. **Amen.**

GET CRAFTY!

Difficulty level

suitable for all ages  for older children

Use these crafts to help communicate how we are all precious to God and welcomed into His family.

1 POP-UP HEART CARDS

You will need: *sheets of card, heart shape to draw around, finger paints, glue*

Preparation: Pre-cut hearts or provide a suitable template.

Each child will need an A4 sheet of card folded in half, and a medium-sized heart made of card.

To make the card:

- Decorate the heart shape by dipping fingers into the paint and dabbing it over the heart shape.
- Let the heart dry, then fold it in half vertically with the painted side *on the outside.*
- Fold the plain sheet of A4 card in half too.
- Carefully fold 2cm of each side of the heart back.
- On the two edges, apply glue and stick them near the centre of the A4 sheet of card so they pop up when opened.

2 ROSETTE

You will need: *cupcake cases, card, ribbons, sticky letters or pens, glue, scissors*

To make the rosette:

- Take three cupcake cases. Squash them flat and glue them directly on top of each other.
- Cut out two circles from the card, one slightly larger than the other.
- Stick the larger circle on top of the cupcake cases, then stick the smaller circle in the middle of the large circle.
- On the back of the cupcake cases add a ribbon (or card cut out to look like a ribbon).
- Decorate it, writing on the words 'God loves me' with stickers or pen.

3 DVD SOCK PUPPETS

You will need: *a sock, googly eyes, wool, ribbon, pipe cleaners, craft balls, fabric glue*

Each child will need a sock and some wool to make their member of the 'Sock' family.

- Make the puppet's hair by wrapping wool round and round your hand. (You will need a good amount.)
- Tie the wool together.
- Cut the woolly hair into a style and stick it to the heel of the sock (i.e. the top of the puppet's head).
- Add googly eyes and a craft ball nose to complete the face.
- Personalise the design by adding ribbons, bows, pipe-cleaner glasses, etc.

I am
God's very special
treasure
1 Peter
2:9
LWC
Little
WORSHIP
Company
AM2

③ God is with me as I grow

In this session, the children will:

- explore the idea that they will grow and change as they get older
- understand that God will never change and will always love and be with them

Hebrews 13:8

Jesus Christ is the same yesterday and today and forever.

ICE-BREAKER

Preparation level

GAME: CATERPILLARS AND BUTTERFLIES 

This is a version of *Duck, Duck, Goose*, but using 'caterpillars' and 'butterflies'.

Sit the children in a large circle. Explain that they are all little caterpillars, waiting to change into big butterflies.

Walk around the outside of the circle, tapping each child lightly on the head and saying "Caterpillar". Eventually, tap one child on the head and call, "Butterfly!" You must run (or flap!) around the circle while the 'butterfly' jumps up and chases you. If you make it back to their spot in the circle, they will now be 'it' and the process starts again.

LITTLE BIG QUESTION

What was your favourite/first toy when you were teeny tiny?

LITTLE BIG IDEA

ILLUSTRATION: GROWING UP 

Preparation You will need to collect some pictures of you and your team when you were younger.

Share some pictures of you and your team, from when you were a baby up to childhood and teenage years. Invite comments on your changing hairstyles and fashions over the years.

Tip: You could run this as a quiz. Can the children tell who the team member is from their baby or childhood picture?

For younger children, you might like to show how 'teddy' has grown up (this will involve a little more preparation).

Preparation: Take some pictures in advance of 'teddy' at different milestones, e.g. in a nappy, learning to ride a bike or scooter, going to school with his book bag, learning to play an instrument, etc.

Show these to the children. Talk about what's happening in the different pictures. How do these pictures connect with the children's own experiences?

LINK TO MESSAGE

Use these photos to introduce the theme of growing up.

MESSAGE

- Have you ever looked back at pictures of you as a baby? How were you different? Can you remember any stories of things you used to do?
- Everybody grows up. And as we do, we change. We definitely look different! But we also change as people.
- As we get bigger, we do new things – for example, go to new schools and learn new things. We like different things. We get new hobbies and meet new friends. But even though *we* change, *God* doesn't.
- We've looked at how God made us and how God loves us. We've seen how God is our wonderful Heavenly Dad who promises to be with us always. That's true right now. It will be true tomorrow, next week, next year and in ten years' time too.
- The Bible says that God doesn't change. Hebrews 13:8 says that Jesus is "the same yesterday and today and forever".
- Because God is always the same, we can completely trust His promises to us. As we grow up, we can be sure that God will always be with us and will always, *always* love us!

LET'S WORSHIP

Song: *Bubble of Praise*

Singalong: *Every Little Hair*

Prayer: **Amazing Me** thank you prayer

LITTLE GROUPS

GOD IS WITH US

You will need: *timeline worksheet (found in appendix), pens and pencils*

Give each child a timeline to fill in. The worksheet encourages them to reflect on happy memories of their life so far and to dream about what the future holds.

At the end of the activity, thank God that He will always be with us and will always love us.

SESSION PRAYER

Dear God, thank you that even though we change, You never will. Thank you that You will be with us as we grow and that You will always love us. **Amen.**

GET CRAFTY!

Difficulty level

suitable for all ages · for older children

God is with us as we grow. Use these crafts to help children remember that as they get bigger, God will be beside them.

1 PAPER PLATE CLOCK

You will need: *paper plates, split pins, colouring pens or paints, sheet of card*

Preparation: You might want to cut out clock hands in advance if using this craft with younger children.

To make the clock:

- Decorate a paper plate with paints or pens.
- Cut two clock hands out of card, one slightly longer than the other.
- Attach the end of each hand to the middle of the clock using a split pin.
- Add numbers or buttons around the clock.

2 FLOWER HEIGHT CHART

You will need: *coloured card, pens, decorating materials, green ribbon*

Preparation: Cut out 'flower' shapes from card or provide a suitable template.

To make the height chart:

- Decorate the flower. (The children might like to write their name or draw a picture of themselves in the middle.)
- Cut a long piece of green ribbon. (**Note:** The ribbon needs to be at least as long as the child, or a little longer if the flower will grow with them.)
- Attach the ribbon to the base of the flower.

The height chart can be attached to a wall at home, at the height of the child. The child can then move the flower up the wall as they grow!

Tip: You could make a 'rocket' version too, using rocket shapes and white ribbon for the jet stream.

3 DVD GIANT TAPE MEASURE

You will need: *sheets of A4 paper, scissors, glue, paint, pens*

To make your giant tape measure:

- Cut along the middle of each of the 3 sheets of paper, lengthways, to make 6 bits of paper.
- Put glue at the top of one sheet and then stick it to the bottom of the next sheet. Repeat until all 6 lengths are stuck together.
- Make marks along the 'tape measure'. You might like to write 'God is with me' at different points along the measure.
- Decorate it. (You might like to try special footprints. Dip the side of your fist in paint and press a shape onto the tape measure. It should look a bit like footprints. To finish it off, paint 'toes' onto each one using fingerprinting.)

Little WORSHIP Company
Jesus Christ is the same
YESTERDAY
and
TODAY
and
FOREVER
Hebrews 13:8
NIV
AM3

4 God asks me to be His friend

In this session, the children will:

- explore the story of God calling Samuel
- understand that we are never too young to know and follow God

1 Timothy 4:12 (MSG)

Don't let anyone put you down because you're young.

ICE-BREAKER

Preparation level

GAME: SIMON SAYS

This game provides a fun opportunity to test out the children's listening skills!

To play the game, you will need a leader ('Simon'). The children begin by standing in a space in front of the leader.

The leader calls out instructions for the children to follow. If they introduce the instruction with "Simon says", then the children must do it. (E.g. "Simon says hop on one leg.")

If the leader does NOT say "Simon says", then the children shouldn't follow the instruction. (E.g. "Lie on the floor.") Any children who do so are out.

Keep playing until you find a winner. To make it more challenging, gradually speed up the instructions.

LITTLE BIG QUESTION

Have you ever been told you were too little for something?

LITTLE BIG IDEA

ILLUSTRATION: GOD'S FRIEND SAMUEL

***You will need:** the **God's Friend Samuel** sheet, found in the appendix*

Explore the calling of Samuel, found in Samuel 3.

To make the story interactive, read the Little Worship Company version found in the appendix. Invite the children to join in with some actions when they hear key words.

With younger children, you might like to sing a song about the Lord calling to Samuel (to the tune of 'Sleeping Bunnies').

Prepare the children by reading the story of Samuel from a children's Bible before 'enacting' the experience in song.

Look at Samuel sleeping 'til the night is through, but God is calling to him, with a job to do
He's so still, that's until... ***(Wake up, Samuel!)***
"Here I am, Lord, here I am – Here I am, Lord, here I am;
Here I am, Lord, here I am – Here I am."

MESSAGE

To introduce this session's Bible verse, you might like to play the song *Even Though I'm Teeny Weeny,* found on the DVD.

- Have you ever been told that you are too little for something? What was it?
- There are some things that we might be too little for. But there is a special something that we are never too small for – and that's knowing God and being His friend!
- Throughout the Bible, there are stories of God talking to children and young people. We've looked at one together: God speaking to Samuel. Even though Samuel was still young, God spoke to him. He wanted Samuel to know Him and follow Him.
- The same is true for us. We've thought about how God made us and how He loves us. We've thought about how God cares for us. But God also wants to talk to us. He wants us to be His friends.
- The Bible says that Jesus told His disciples, "Let the little children come to me" (Matthew 19:14). He knew how special children were to God and wanted them, as well as grown-ups, to hear what God had to say to them.
- Whether we're big or small, we are incredibly important to God. And we're never too young to learn how to listen to God and follow Him.

LET'S WORSHIP

Song: *Be With You*
Singalong: *Every Little Hair*
Prayer: Amazing Me thank you prayer

LITTLE GROUPS

'SLEEPING LIONS' PRAYERS

We are never too young to learn how to listen to God. These 'sleeping lions' prayers give children the space to hear from Him themselves.

Invite the children to lie on the floor while the team pray over them.

Ask the children to imagine a whiteboard. What would God be writing or drawing on it to them? What do they think that means?

Invite the children to share anything they heard or saw.

At the end of the time, thank God that He is with us and asks us to be His friends.

SESSION PRAYER

Dear God, thank you that we are never too small to be Your friend! Help us to keep our eyes open to see You, and our ears open to hear what You are asking us to do. **Amen.**

GET CRAFTY!

Difficulty level
suitable for all ages · for older children

Every one of us is important to God. Use these crafts to help children remember that, young or old, God invites us to be His friends.

1 THREAD PEOPLE

You will need: *a hole punch, thread, pens, card, shiny ribbon*

Optional: *buttons, decorating materials*

Each child will need a piece of card, shaped like a person. (Make this by drawing round a gingerbread man shape.)

To make the thread people:

- Punch holes around the edges of the cardboard person.
- Thread wool or string through the holes.
- Decorate it with buttons or stickers, or simply colour it in.

As you model your 'little people', remind the children that no one is too small to know God.

2 'VIP' CROWN

You will need: *a paper plate, sparkly decorations (like stickers, gems and glitter), cotton wool, pens (prep: craft knife, ruler)*

Preparation: Make the 'crowns' in advance. Take a paper plate. Using a ruler and craft knife, cut a line across the centre of the plate, leaving a 3cm margin on each side. Repeat 3 times. The lines should cross over each other at the centre point, so that you have divided the plate into 8 small triangles.

Each child will need a prepared paper plate. To make the crown:

- Decorate the plate using any materials you might have.
- Once finished, fold the triangles up to make the crown.
- Add cotton wool to the base for effect.

As the children wear the crown, remind them that even though they are small, they are a 'very important person' to God.

3 DVD FRIENDS BUNTING

You will need: *a roll of brown paper, scissors, pens, paper, decorating materials*

Preparation: Cut lengths of brown paper, 15cm or so in height. Create a 'person' template.

Each child will need a length of brown paper.

To make the friends bunting:

- Fold the brown paper back and forth, in a concertina.
- Draw a person shape on top of the paper. **NB: The arms need to touch the folded edges** to ensure that they remain joined when the paper is unfolded.
- Cut around the person shape. Once opened, there should be a string of friends!
- Decorate the paper friends. Design clothes out of paper or fabric and stick them onto the paper people, or use stickers and pens.

As you make this craft, remind the children how God wants everyone to be His friend.

I'm never too small to be God's friend!
1 Timothy 4:12 LWC
Me and God

5 God made me for an adventure with Him

In this session, the children will:

- explore the idea of being made for a purpose
- understand that God calls us to follow Him and that we can discover what this means by reading the Bible

Ephesians 2:10 (LWC)

We are God's best artwork!

ICE-BREAKER

Preparation level

zero easy medium

GAME: AMAZING MACHINES

Break the children into teams. Call out an invention. The children must work together to make the shape of it using their bodies.

Suggestions: a TV, an aeroplane, a car

LITTLE BIG QUESTION

If you could make up a brand new invention, what would it be?

LITTLE BIG IDEA

ILLUSTRATION: MOST MARVELLOUS INVENTIONS 

You will need: *some everyday items from around the house which you could show the children*

Tell the children that you have been shopping and you want to show them what you bought. Bring a few items out – explain that they looked nice but you're not entirely sure what they're for. For example:

- a kettle – it has a hole in the top. Perhaps it's a vase for flowers?
- a melon – it's big and round. Maybe it's a football?
- a picture book – it's big and lightweight. Maybe it's a fan for hot days?

Let the children help/correct you.

Alternative for older children

You will need: *plenty of small building blocks or Meccano-style construction sets*

Break the children into small groups. Give each group some building blocks. Give them five minutes to 'build' a version of their favourite invention – or something brand new!

At the end of the challenge, invite them to present their creations to each other. Commend them for their creativity.

LINK TO MESSAGE

The world is full of marvellous inventions. But the greatest, most marvellous things ever made are sitting in this room – that's us!

You might like to show the **session Bible verse**, found on the DVD, here. 

MESSAGE

- The world is full of marvellous inventions – objects made to do incredible things. (You might refer to some of your favourites.)
- The Bible says that God made us. We are His amazing work of art and we are incredibly special to Him.
- But the Bible also says that we were made for a reason. Ephesians 2:10 says, "We are God's handiwork" – that is, His work of art – "created in Christ Jesus to do good works".
- In other words, God made us to do amazing things – things that make Him happy and will change the world.
- One of the ways we can find out about God's big plans for us is by reading the Bible. It's God's special instruction book for our life. We can get to know God and what it means to live for Him by reading it.
- We might not know exactly what God has in store for us as we get bigger, but as we look in the Bible, we'll know which way to go.

LET'S WORSHIP

Song: *Be Thou My Vision*

Singalong: *Be Brave and Courageous*

Prayer: **Amazing Me** thank you prayer

LITTLE GROUPS

GOD'S GREAT ADVENTURE

You will need: *a big sheet of paper, pens*

One of the best ways we can discover what we were made to be and do is by looking at Jesus.

Talk to the children about what they know about Jesus.

- Which stories do you know about Jesus?
- What do you think they tell us about living for God?

Record the ideas on the paper – either in words or pictures.

SESSION PRAYER

Dear God, thank you that You made every one of us and that You really, really love what You made! Thank you that You have big plans for us and that You will always be with us. **Amen.**

GET CRAFTY!

Difficulty level
suitable for all ages / for older children

God made us for an adventure with Him. Use these 'adventure inventions' to reflect on what a life with God looks like.

1 BOTTLE ROCKET (for older children)

You will need: *an old plastic bottle, scissors, paint, card, foil, kitchen roll tubes, glue/sticky tape*

Preparation: If using this with younger children, you may want to cut the bottles and cardboard circles in advance.

Each child will need one plastic bottle.

To make the rocket:

- Cut the top off the bottle. Paint the bottle in a bright colour.
- Cut a circle of card and cut it into the middle. Curl it into a cone shape and tape it. Cover it in shiny foil and glue it to the top of the rocket.
- Cut the kitchen roll into little tubes. Paint them black to make the boosters. Tape them to the bottom of the rocket.
- Cut some 'fins' out of card. Stick these to the side to complete the rocket.
- You might want to add more detail and decoration – e.g. doors and windows.

As you make the rocket, talk about the different adventures the children have been on, or would like to go on. Share stories about your own 'God adventures'.

2 BIG FOOT STOMPERS (for older children)

You will need: *cardboard, decorating materials, ribbon*

Preparation: You will need to create a giant foot template in advance.

To make the stompers:

- Take two sheets of cardboard. Draw an enormous foot on each one from the template and cut it out.
- Decorate the feet.
- Make two slits in each one (about the same width as a child's foot). Thread a piece of 30cm ribbon through each slot to make a strap so the feet can be worn.

Tip: Why not create a mini assault course with cushions and boxes and see if the children can walk through using their special shoes?

Use this craft to help the children remember that God's great adventure starts with following in Jesus' footsteps.

3 JUNK MODELLING INVENTIONS (suitable for all ages)

You will need: *decorating materials and assorted 'junk' e.g. plastic bottles, cardboard tubes and boxes, plastic lids, etc.*

Let the children invent anything they want from the materials on the table.

Use this craft to help the children remember that they were made by God to do wonderful things for Him.

We are God's best artwork!
Draw *your* best artwork here!
Ephesians 2:10
LWC
Little WORSHIP Company
AM5

6 God's love for me never runs out

In this session, the children will:

- explore the story of the Lost Sheep
- understand that we are and always will be precious to God; and that God will always forgive us when we make mistakes

Zephaniah 3:17

He will take great delight in you... [He] will rejoice over you with singing.

ICE-BREAKER

Preparation level

zero easy medium

GAME: SPOT THE SHEEP

You will need: *plastic chairs and lots of blankets/sheets*

Preparation: Create a big circle using plastic chairs. Drape blankets over clusters of chairs, so that children can hide behind the chairs. Leave some gaps within the circle.

To play the game you will need a 'shepherd' to sit in the centre of the circle. The rest of the group are all sheep.

The aim of the game is for the shepherd to spot their 'sheep'. The sheep crawl around the outside of the circle, hiding from the shepherd. The shepherd keeps their eyes and ears open to see if they can work out where the different sheep are. (The gaps in the circle provide an extra challenge for the sheep – and help for the shepherd!)

When the shepherd correctly identifies a sheep's location, that 'sheep' becomes the shepherd in the centre of the circle. (The former 'shepherd' then joins the sheep.)

LITTLE BIG QUESTION

Have you ever found something that you thought you'd lost? How did it feel?

LITTLE BIG IDEA

ILLUSTRATION: LOST!

You will need: *the* ***Lost!*** *worksheet, found in the appendix*

Preparation: You will need to hide an item somewhere in the session venue in advance.

Enact a live, reimagined version of Jesus' parable of the lost sheep/lost coin with the children, using the guidance found in the appendix. (These stories are found in Luke 15.)

LINK TO MESSAGE

Jesus told stories to help people understand how precious they were to God – for example, the lost sheep or lost coin.

Whatever happens, or whatever we do, nothing will stop God from loving us or finding us if we get into trouble.

You might like to show the **session Bible verse**, found on the DVD, here. 

MESSAGE

- We've looked at how precious we are to God: how He made us and loves us like an amazing parent.
- We've also thought about how God asks us all to be His special friends. God loves to talk to us and wants to take us on an amazing adventure with Him.
- But there are times when we *aren't* very good friends to God. There are times when we don't listen to Him, or when we do things that hurt Him or other people. (You might give some practical examples.) It's like we walk away from God, and that makes Him really sad.
- But the Bible also says that no matter what we do, God loves us just the same. He doesn't get cross with us and say He doesn't want to be friends any more. He loves us and His love for us never, ever runs out.
- Zephaniah 3:17 says, "He will take great delight in you... He will rejoice over you with singing." It's a picture of how much God loves us – that when we come to Him and say sorry, God is so happy that He hugs us and sings a song over us to celebrate!

LET'S WORSHIP

Song: *You're Beautiful*

Singalong: *Be Brave and Courageous*

Prayer: **Amazing Me** thank you prayer

LITTLE GROUPS

BUBBLE PRAYERS

You will need: *bubble mixture*

Invite the children to get comfortable, away from any distraction.

Explain that God loves us and will always forgive us when we say sorry.

Take a moment to be quiet. Is there anything the children want to say sorry to God for?

Either blow some bubbles or invite the children to blow some bubbles. Tell the children that as the bubbles pop, they can be sure that those things are gone and God has forgiven them.

SESSION PRAYER

Dear God, we're really sorry for the times we make bad choices. Thank you that we are Your precious children, and that there's nothing in the world that stops You from loving us. **Amen.**

GET CRAFTY!

Difficulty level
suitable for all ages | for older children

God's great love never runs out. Use these crafts to help the children explore how much God cares for us.

1 GOD'S BIG HUG

You will need: *card, brown paper roll, paint and/or colouring pens, glue, scissors*

Preparation: Cut long strips (about 3cm wide) from the brown paper roll.

To make the 'hug':

- Create two hands. You could make these by coating the children's hands in paint and printing them onto the card. For a less messy option, the children could simply draw round their hands and cut them out.
- Take two strips of brown paper. Fold them over each other in a concertina style until you reach the end.
- Stick the hands to each end to complete your 'hug'.

TIP: If using paint, remember to provide a bowl of soapy water and towels nearby.

As you do the craft, think about what a hug means. Draw the parallel with how much God loves us. When we do something wrong and we say sorry a hug helps us to remember we are still loved. God loves us always even when we get things wrong. When we say sorry to God we know He will always forgive us.

2 'LOVE BUG' STAINED-GLASS WINDOW

You will need: *sticky-back plastic sheets, various colours of tissue paper (cut up into small squares), 'love bug' shapes, coloured craft paper, black craft paper (in strips), glue*

Preparation: You will need a 'heart' template to make the 'love bugs'.

To make the stained-glass window:

- Stick squares of coloured tissue paper onto a sheet of sticky-back plastic.
- Make a 'love bug' from craft paper, using the heart template. Place the 'love bug' into the centre of the sticky-back plastic.
- 'Close' the stained-glass window by placing another sheet of sticky-back plastic over the top (i.e. sticky side down).
- To finish off, make a frame out of the black craft paper strips and stick it to the 'window'.

Invite the children to put this in their bedroom window at home. When the sun shines through, they can remember how much God loves them!

3 WOOLLY HEART

You will need: *strong card, scissors, colourful wool – ideally quite thick*

Preparation: Each child will need a heart frame. To make this, cut a large heart shape from card and then cut a smaller heart shape from the middle of it.

To make the woolly heart, simply wrap the wool around the cardboard frame until it is completely covered.

Older children may like to plait some separate strands together to make a ribbon. Attach this to the heart, so that the children can hang it up and remember God's great love for them. He loves us always, no matter what we do or say, and He will never stop loving us.

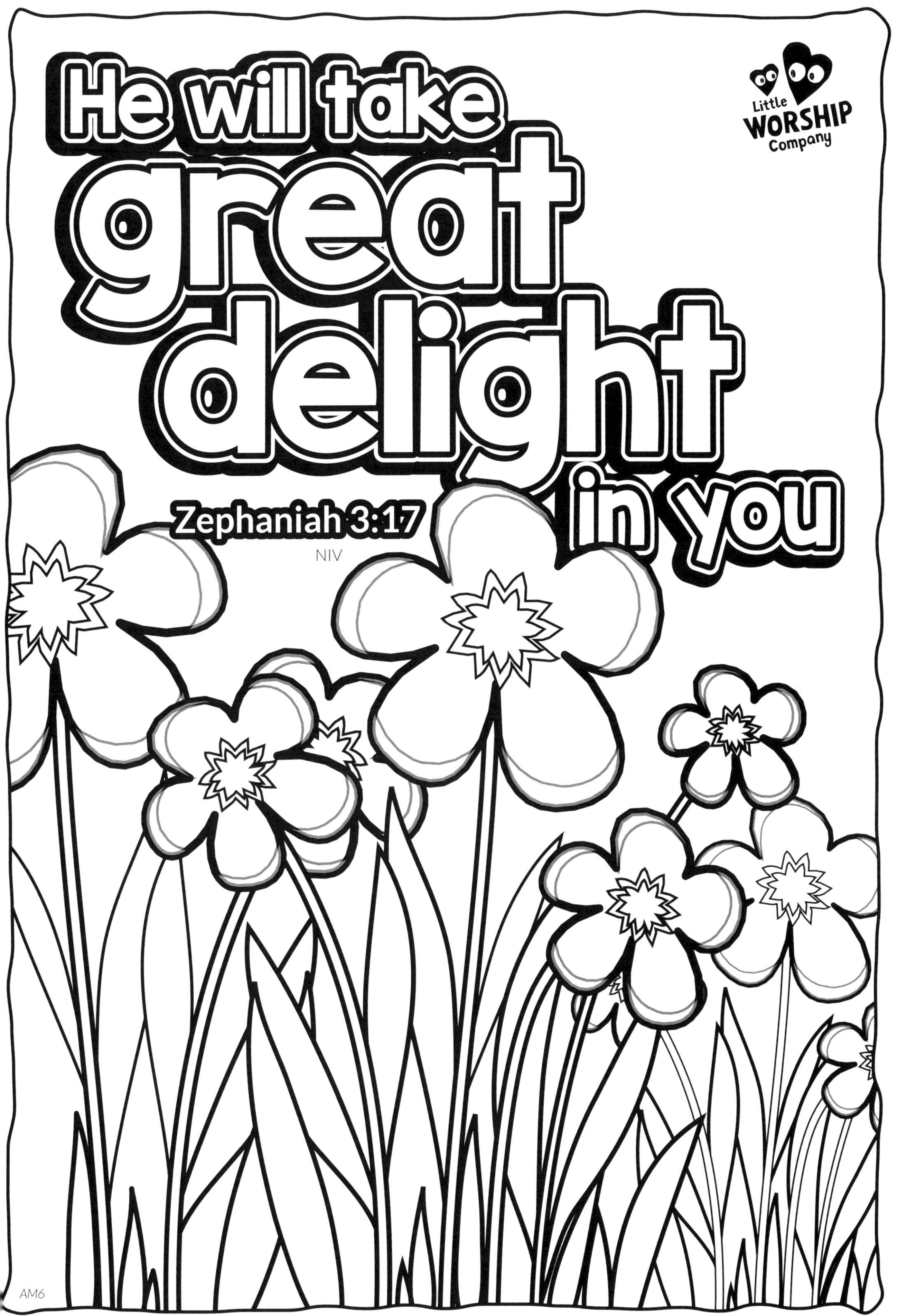
He will take great delight in you
Zephaniah 3:17
NIV
Little WORSHIP Company
AM6

7 God makes me brave

In this session, the children will:

- explore the story of Joshua crossing the Jordan
- understand that God is always with us and that He will give us His courage

Joshua 1:9 (LWC)

Be strong and be courageous. Do not be afraid or troubled, for the Lord your God is with you wherever you go!

ICE-BREAKER

Preparation level

zero easy medium

GAME: CROSSING THE RIVER

Preparation: You will need to assemble various materials for an obstacle course – for example, hoops to jump into or through, a net or parachute to scramble under, benches to walk over, etc.

Break the children into teams. Explain that the room is a wide river that they need to cross. Demonstrate how to 'cross the river' by completing all the different obstacles you have assembled.

Run the race as a relay – i.e. when one team member gets to the other side, the next one begins, until the whole team has completed the challenge.

LITTLE BIG QUESTION

What's the bravest thing you've ever done?

LITTLE BIG IDEA

ILLUSTRATION: JOSHUA AND THE DEEP, WIDE RIVER

You will need: *a large blue sheet, stones, the* ***Joshua and the Deep, Wide River*** *sheet (found in the appendix)*

Read the **Little Worship Company** version of Joshua 3-4. Invite the children to join in with the actions.

LINK TO MESSAGE

You might like to show the **session Bible verse**, found on the DVD, here. 

MESSAGE

- Can you think of a time when somebody asked you to do something, and you had to be really brave?
- We've looked at how God made us and loves us, and how He invites us to join Him on a big adventure. But even though this is really exciting, sometimes it can feel a bit scary too.
- This was how Joshua felt. God asked Joshua to take the Israelites into a brand new land. But there were all sorts of obstacles in the way. Joshua was scared.
- God promised that He was with Joshua, and that He would help him. God said, "Be strong and be courageous. Do not be afraid or troubled, for the Lord your God is with you wherever you go." (Joshua 1:9)
- This promise is true for us too. As we get older, we will face new challenges – and we might not always feel good enough or brave enough to do them. (Give some examples.)
- But we can be sure that God is always with us. He's big and strong. And because He promises to help us, we can be really brave and go for it!

LET'S WORSHIP

Song: *Oceans*

Singalong: *Be Brave and Courageous*

Prayer: **Amazing Me** thank you prayer

LITTLE GROUPS

PEBBLE PRAYERS

You will need: *either real stones or paper cut-outs of stones (a template can be found in the appendix)*

In the story of Joshua (Joshua 4), the people of Israel take stones from the Jordan riverbed to remind them how God helped them cross over.

Encourage the children to think of a time when God has answered their prayer, or when they knew God was with them, helping them to be brave. Let them write it down on a pebble (real or paper), or simply hold the pebble as they think/talk about it.

You might like to make your own 'memorial' by assembling the stones. As you look at the memorial together, thank God that He will always be with us and that we don't need to be scared when He's beside us and helping us.

SESSION PRAYER

Dear God, thank you that we never need to be scared, because You're always with us. Thank you that You make us brave. **Amen.**

GET CRAFTY!

Difficulty level

suitable for all ages   for older children

Use these crafts to reflect on how God helps us to be brave.

1 MEDAL

You will need: *air-drying clay, cookie cutters, paints, ribbons*

Preparation: A week before you make these medals, you will need to make round discs from air-drying clay. You could cut out a circle with a cookie cutter. Push a pencil through at the top to make a hole. Leave to dry for 5-7 days.

For the actual craft, let the children decorate their medal however they wish. Thread a ribbon through the medal so that it can be worn.

2 SUPERHERO CAPE

You will need: *an old T-shirt, fabric pens, fabric glue, felt pieces*

To make the cape:

- An adult will need to cut around the front of the neck of the T-shirt, then down the back sides to make a cape.
- Decorate the T-shirt with fabric pens. Cut out shapes from the felt and glue them onto the T-shirt to finish off your superhero cape.

As you make the superhero craft(s), talk about how we can be even braver than a superhero because God is with us.

3 SUPERHERO WRISTBANDS

You will need: *cardboard tubes, paints, decorating materials*

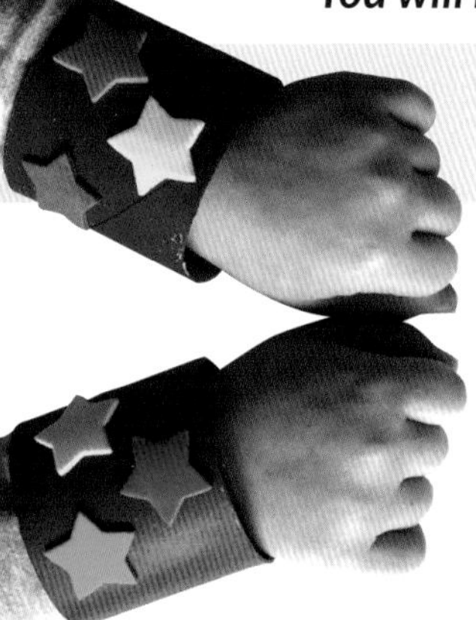

Preparation: Cut the tubes in half (widthways) and cut a slit lengthways so that they can be easily worn on the wrists.

Each child will need two cardboard tubes to make their cuffs. Invite them to paint them a bright superhero colour, before decorating with stickers and pens.

Joshua 1:9
LWC
Be strong and brave:
God is with you!
Little
WORSHIP
Company
AM7

8 God makes me strong

In this session, the children will:

- explore the concept of 'strength'
- understand that God is with us and loves us and gives us His strength

Philippians 4:13 (LWC)

I can do anything – Jesus has made me strong!

ICE-BREAKER

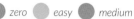

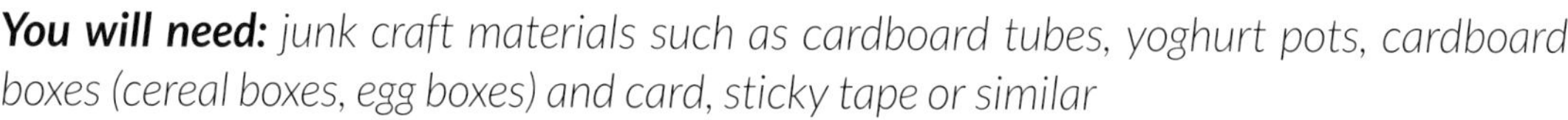

GAME: BUILD-A-BRIDGE CHALLENGE

You will need: *junk craft materials such as cardboard tubes, yoghurt pots, cardboard boxes (cereal boxes, egg boxes) and card, sticky tape or similar*

Break the children into teams. Explain that they need to create a bridge strong enough to carry different items out of the materials they are given.

Tip: To make it fair, give each team a 'pack' comprising the same materials.

Give the children 5 to 10 minutes to make their bridges. At the end, see how strong they are. For example, will they hold a small toy car, or an apple, or a mug?

LITTLE BIG QUESTION

Who is the strongest person that you know? What have you seen them carry?

LITTLE BIG IDEA

ILLUSTRATION: BEACH BALL

You will need: *a deflated beach ball, a pump (electric or manual)*

Ask the children if they would like to play a game of catch.

Present your deflated ball. Try to throw the ball to somebody. Hopefully they will express some disappointment that the ball is not as it should be – and that you can't play.

Find your solution: you have a pump. Plug it in and inflate the ball in front of the children. Marvel at the difference it has made. Play a few rounds of catch.

LINK TO MESSAGE

Sometimes we can feel a little bit like the deflated beach ball. But God promises to make us strong. He puts His strength inside of us, so that there's nothing we can't do.

You might like to show the **session Bible verse**, found on the DVD, here. 

MESSAGE

- The Bible says, "I can do anything – Jesus has made me strong!" (Philippians 4:13). But what does that mean? Does it mean we'll be able to carry a big box of toys upstairs by ourselves? Will we be able to carry our big brother or sister, or our grandma?
- When the Bible talks about strength, it means having something inside us which makes our heart feel strong.
- Sometimes, we might feel sad or worried about things which happen to us. (We can feel a bit like the deflated beach ball.)
- But the Bible promises that God is with us (see Joshua 1:9). When we choose to be friends with God, He comes to live in our hearts. He gives us His strength, making us strong on the inside.
- If there is ever anything that is worrying you, remember that God is always near and always listening. There's nothing too big or too small for Him.
- Tell God about it – He loves to help! He is really strong, and He gives us all the strength we need. With God, there's nothing we can't face.

LET'S WORSHIP

Song: *This is Living*

Singalong: *Be Brave and Courageous*

Prayer: **Amazing Me** thank you prayer

LITTLE GROUPS

IN GOD'S HANDS

You will need: *paper, pens*

Invite the children to draw around their hands on the paper provided. Explain that wherever we go and whatever we do, we are safe in God's big hands.

Invite them to draw themselves in the middle of the handprint, to remind them how much God cares for them.

SESSION PRAYER

Thank you, God, that no matter what we go through, You always help us.

Thank you that You make us strong! **Amen.**

GET CRAFTY!

Difficulty level

 suitable for all ages  for older children

Use these crafts to help the children reflect on how God makes them strong.

1 FORK PRINT LION

You will need: *yellow/orange paint, paper plates, forks, googly eyes, glue, chunky black felt tips*

- Take a paper plate and a fork. Dip the fork into yellow and orange paint and print all around the plate to make the lion's mane.
- Draw a triangle nose, lines for the mouth and add googly eyes to finish your brave lion.

Use this craft to talk about courage and strength. We are stronger and bolder than even a lion when God is with us!

2  STRONG SHIELD 

You will need: *A4 or A3 card, pens and pencils, scissors, decorating material (e.g. tissue paper, foil, stickers), strips of card, sticky tape*

Preparation: Depending on the age of your group, you might like to create a shield template in advance.

To make the shield:

- Fold a piece of card in half longways.
- Draw one half of a shield from the centre-fold to the edge of the card. Cut it out. When it opens, you should have a symmetrical shield shape.
- Decorate the shield.
- To finish it off, take a strip of card. Fold the card twice, at about 2cm from both ends. Stick these flaps onto the back of the shield so that you have a handle.

As you make this craft, talk about how God's special peace is like a shield for our hearts, making us strong on the inside.

3 IN GOD'S HANDS

You will need: *large card, paints, corn on the cob*

Preparation: If using with younger children, create large hand shapes from A4 or A3 card in advance. Make a template for older children to use themselves.

To make this picture:

- Take (or draw and cut out) a large hand shape.
- Dip a corn on the cob in paint and roll it over the hand shape to make some textured paintwork.
- Once finished, draw a picture of yourself in the middle of the hand, to show how God holds us and all the situations we face.

Use this craft to help the children to visualise how God is always with us and carries us in good times and tough times.

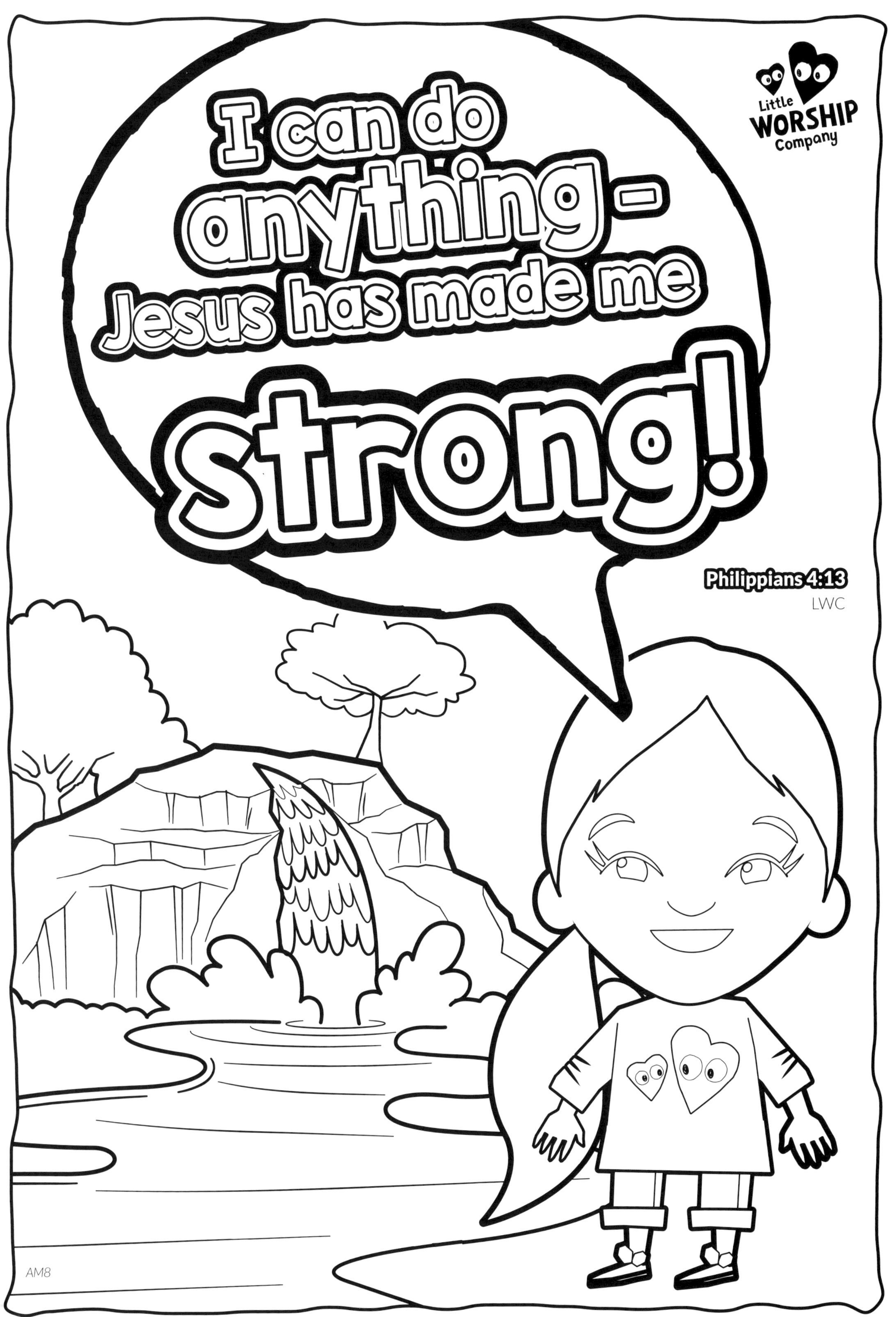
Little WORSHIP Company
I can do anything - Jesus has made me strong!
Philippians 4:13
LWC
AM8

AMAZING ME
All-age worship

At the end of the curriculum course, you may like to lead a Sunday morning, all-age worship service on the curriculum's theme, inviting the children to participate in leading it.

Follow or adapt the service plan below as appropriate for your congregation.

WELCOME

Welcome the congregation to the service.

OPENING PRAYER

Dear God, You are so awesome! Thank you that You made us, that You know us, and that You love us completely.

We really want to meet with You [this morning] to find out more about You and about all that You have in store for us. Open our eyes to see You and our mouths to praise You today. **Amen.**

WORSHIP

Sing a couple of **songs** from the **Amazing Me** DVD. 

Say this **child-friendly prayer** together. Invite the children – big ones as well as little ones! – to join in with some actions as you read.

ALL-AGE LITURGY

Thank you, God, for making me.

Thank you for my jumping legs.

Thank you for my strong arms.

Thank you for my listening ears.

Thank you for my blinking eyes.

Thank you for my nose that can smell.

Thank you for my full tummy.

Thank you for my cool hair.

Thank you for my HUGE smile.

Thank you, God, for amazing me!

Amen.

CHILDREN'S SLOT

Invite the children to the front to talk about the different things they have learnt over the last few weeks. They might like to share some of the crafts they have made, or any memory verses they have learnt.

The children may also like to sing an **Amazing Me singalong song.**  Perhaps they could teach it to the adults!

WORD

Read one or more of the suggested **Bible readings** (or choose your own). Invite a range of readers – young and old – to do this.

- **1 Peter 2:4-10** We are chosen by God and called to do amazing things for Him.
- **Psalm 139:1-16** God made us, knows us, and is always with us.
- **John 15:9-17** God loves each one of us and asks us to share that love with others.

MESSAGE

Share the suggested message below or create your own.

Key Bible passage: 1 Peter 2:4-10

Key message: Each one of us is incredibly precious to God – His special treasure.

Preparation: You will need to research relevant examples to support the three points below.

INTRODUCTION

Introduce the theme of 'precious things'. You may like to do one or more of the following:

- Ask the congregation about the most precious 'treasure' they own. What is it? Why is it so special?
- Show something that is incredibly precious to you and explain why it's so precious.
- Look at examples of conventionally valuable things – cars, art, etc. You may like to turn this into a quiz by asking the congregation to guess their value.

REFLECTION

- Over the last few weeks the children have been exploring the idea of **Amazing Me.** 1 Peter 2:9 (LWC) says that we are "God's special treasure". We are all incredibly precious. But what makes something precious?
- Something is precious **because of who made it.** *[Share an example of this – e.g. sheets of music handwritten by Mozart, a sketch by da Vinci.]* In the same way, we are precious because we are made by God. Psalm 139:14 says we are "fearfully and wonderfully made" – God's own unique work of art. That makes us special!

- Something is precious **because of what somebody is willing to pay for it.** *[Choose an example of an item recently sold at auction for a record price.]* In the same way, we are precious because we were bought at a high price by God. The Bible teaches that Jesus was willing to give His life to make a way for us to be friends with God. That makes us very special!
- Finally, something is precious **because of who it belongs to.** *[Show an item. Explain that it doesn't look like much – but what difference would it make to know that it belonged to the Queen, and she very much wanted it back?]* In the same way, we are precious because we are now part of God's family. The Bible says that God calls us His own dear children. We belong to God. And that makes us very, very special indeed.

PRAYERS

WONDERFULLY MADE

Use this activity as a way of prayerfully responding to the message.

You will need: pens, paper people

Preparation: Give out pens and little people cut-outs.

- Invite the congregation to reflect on what they have heard. What is God saying to them, and about them, this morning? It might be a Bible verse, a promise, or a command.
- Ask them to write it on their person and then decorate it to look like themselves.
- These can be taken home as a personal encouragement or displayed and prayed over in the church.

FINGERPRINT FAMILY

Every single person on this earth is incredibly precious to God – His special 'treasure'. Use this activity as a commitment to share God's love with others.

You will need: *a roll of paper, ink pads, pens*

Preparation: Roll out the paper at the front of the church. Put ink pads on a table nearby.

- Reflect on how God has made us. Everyone is special; each of us is unique. A sign of this is our fingerprints. No two fingerprints are the same!
- Reflect on how everybody on the planet is made by God and is precious to Him – and it's our job, as His followers, to share that good news with others.
- Invite the congregation to come to the front as a response to that call. Invite them to make a fingerprint on the paper. This then becomes the 'head' of a little stick person which they can draw on afterwards.
- You should end up with the whole church represented on the paper. Think about how God has made each of us with unique personalities, gifts and talents, but has brought us together, as His church, to share His love and hope in the world.
- Pray into the words of Ephesians 2:10: that God will use your church – individually and together – to do the 'good works that He prepared in advance' for you to do in Christ Jesus.

WORSHIP

Sing one or two **songs** from the **Amazing Me** DVD. (You may like to take up an offering here and/or say the Lord's Prayer together.)

BLESSING AND DISMISSAL

Formally close the service.

CLOSING BLESSING

May the God who made us, knows us and loves us be with us today and always. **Amen.**

Picture Frame

Create a picture of yourself. Draw yourself with something that's precious to you or doing something you love.

"THANK YOU, GOD. I am brilliantly and marvellously made." (Psalm 139:14)

PLAY-DOUGH RECIPE

You will need:

- 8 tbsp plain flour
- 2 tbsp table salt
- 2 tsp cream of tartar
- 60ml warm water
- Food colouring
- 1 tbsp vegetable oil

To make the play dough:

1. Mix together ingredients in a bowl.
2. Once mixed, tip out onto a lightly flour-dusted surface and knead until smooth.
3. Store in an airtight container in the fridge.

Amazing Me: Session 3: Timeline worksheet

My Amazing Life

Wherever we go, God will be with us...

My name is ....

I was born on ....

Draw **your first house** here:

Draw **your first school** here:

What do you like **doing at school?**

....

What would you like to **become when you're older?** Write or draw it here:

What's the **most exciting place** you've been to?

....

....

Your **favourite way to spend the day** right now:

1 ....

2 ....

3 ....

Your **favourite people** right now:

1 ....

2 ....

3 ....

Which **place or places would you like to visit** when you're older?

....

....

....

....

GOD'S FRIEND SAMUEL

BASED ON 1 SAMUEL 3

Read the story of God calling to Samuel with the children. Encourage them to join in with the following actions and words when they hear some key phrases. (You might like to practise them first!)

KEY PHRASES AND ACTIONS:

LEADER – story phrase	***CHILDREN*** – *response*
"Samuel… lay/was lying on the floor."	*Lie down on the floor and look sleepy.*
"Samuel got up."	*Sit up and stretch arms, as if waking up.*
"Samuel said…"	*Say together, "HERE I AM!"*
"Eli said, 'I didn't call you.'"	*Wag a finger and say, "No, no, no."*

THE STORY

Once there was a boy named Samuel. He lived in the temple, God's special house, with an old priest called Eli, helping him to serve God each day.

Samuel used to sleep in the temple. One night, **Samuel was lying down on the floor.** Suddenly, he heard a voice calling, "Samuel! Samuel!" **Samuel got up.** He went to find the priest, Eli, who was also asleep. And **Samuel said:**

"HERE I AM! You called me."

But **Eli said, "I didn't call you.** ["No, no, no."] Go back to bed." So Samuel went back and **lay down on the floor.**

But again, Samuel heard a voice calling, "Samuel! Samuel!" **Samuel got up.** Again, he went to find the priest, Eli. And **Samuel said:**

"HERE I AM! You called me."

But **Eli said, "I didn't call you.** ["No, no, no."] Go back to bed." So Samuel went back and **lay down on the floor.**

A third time Samuel heard a voice calling, "Samuel! Samuel!" **Samuel got up.** And a third time he went to find the priest, Eli. And **Samuel said:**

"HERE I AM! You called me."

But this time old Eli realised who was calling to Samuel. It was God. "Next time you hear the voice," Eli said, "You must say, 'Speak, Lord, for your servant is listening.'"

So Samuel went back and **lay down on the floor.** And God called again, "Samuel! Samuel!" **Samuel got up and said,** "HERE I AM. Speak, Lord, for your servant is listening."

And God told Samuel about the many amazing things He was going to do.

REFLECTION

No one is too little to know God. He is always speaking to us. We just need to learn how to listen!

'LOST!' AM6

A contemporary version of the 'lost' parables found in Luke 15:1-10 (the Lost Sheep and the Lost Coin).

For younger children, you may like to re-enact the story of the Lost Sheep using soft toys.

You will need: *some soft toys, music*

Preparation: Hide one of your toys somewhere in the session venue.

- Introduce your soft toys to the children.
- Call each one by name. Talk about how special they are. (Perhaps share a fun fact or anecdote about them!)
- Suddenly realise that one is missing. Where has it gone? Search around for the missing toy. Explain what it looks like and why it is so special to you.
- Get the children involved. Search high and low around the venue for your lost toy.
- When you find it, lead everybody in a big party. You might like to play some party tunes to celebrate!

For older children, let them enjoy counting up items and discovering that something is missing.

You will need: *a collection of items (e.g. CDs or DVDs, or anything you have a lot of), party music*

Preparation: Hide a missing item from your collection somewhere in the venue.

- Introduce the children to your 'collection'. Explain why you're so proud of it/why it's special to you. Make sure you tell the children how many items you have in your collection. (Pick a round number to make it easy on the children.)
- Invite the children to help you count your collection – just to make sure it's all there.
- Divide your collection up and ask the children to count them – e.g. give individual children or groups a collection of 10 items to count. Make sure that one group gets one item less than the rest.
- Let the children help total up the items. Act surprised to find that one is missing. Ask the children to count their pile again, to see if there was a mistake.
- Lead the children in a treasure hunt to find the missing item.
- Celebrate when it's discovered by playing some party music and singing and dancing together.

JOSHUA AND THE DEEP, WIDE RIVER

BASED ON JOSHUA 3 AND 4

You will need:

- *a large, blue sheet and a couple of volunteers to hold it*
- *12 large stones (either real stones or paper cut-outs)*

To set the scene, *place a blue sheet on the ground so that it looks like a river. Ask a couple of adults to stand by each end. They will need to shuffle the sheet and move it into different positions throughout the story.*

Sit the children on the 'edge' of the river – i.e. all on one side of the sheet. They will be the Israelites in the story and will cross over at the relevant point.

THE STORY

God had promised His people that they would have a special land to live in. For years and years they'd been walking around in the desert, longing to reach the Promised Land.

Then one day, God called a man named Joshua. "Get ready," God said. "The time has come for you to cross over the River Jordan and into your new home."

Joshua felt scared. The river was deep and wide. How on earth would they cross?

[Shuffle the blue sheet to make small waves. Lift it gently to make bigger waves. Encourage the children to make wave actions with their hands.]

But God said to Joshua, "Be strong and courageous. Do not be afraid. Do not be discouraged, for the Lord your God will be with you wherever you go." And so Joshua told God's people to get ready.

A few days later, God's people walked down to the edge of the river Jordan. As they looked out at the rushing water, they felt scared. The river was deep and wide. How on earth would they cross?

[Lift the blue sheet to make waves. Encourage the children to make big wave actions with their arms and hands.]

But Joshua told them to trust God. He was with them. God's priests carried a precious box called the Ark of the Covenant in front of the people.

[Leader walks to the edge of the sheet.]

As soon as the priests put their feet into the river Jordan, it stopped flowing. The water piled up in a heap, leaving dry ground.

[Leader puts foot to the water's edge. The volunteers holding the sheet need to get up and rotate or fold the sheet so that there is now 'dry ground' in front of the water.]

One by one, the people of God crossed over the riverbed and landed safely on the other side.

[Invite the children to walk past the sheet, across to the other side. As they do so, scatter some stones onto the 'riverbed'.]

God said to Joshua, "Pick twelve people. Tell them to go and pick up twelve stones from the riverbed." And he did.

[Count out 12 children and ask them to collect the stones. If you have fewer than 12, invite all the children to help you.]

The people collected the stones and made a tower where the priests had been standing when the water stopped flowing.

[Either stack the stones or attach them to a wall using sticky tack.]

And for many years, whenever God's people saw that tower, they would remember that God was with them.

REFLECTION

In the story, Joshua felt scared. God's people felt scared too. Why?
(The river seemed impossible to cross/dangerous, etc.)

There was one important thing which made them brave. Do you remember what it was?
(Knowing that God was with them.)

Prayer Pebble

Think about a time when God has answered your prayer.
Write it inside the stone.

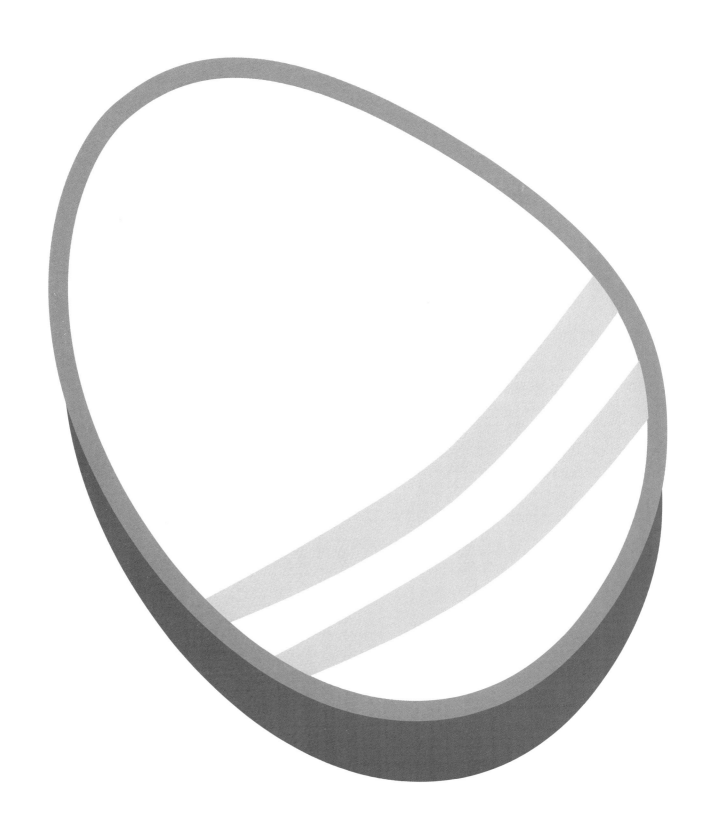

Beautiful World Bible curriculum

BEAUTIFUL WORLD

Our world is amazing! **Beautiful World** takes children on a journey through the creation story, inspiring wonder in the incredible world they live in and helping them to see the God who made, knows and loves it – and who made, knows and loves them too.

1 GOD MADE THE LIGHT

In this session, the children will:

- explore what makes light amazing
- understand it as made by God

God spoke: "Light!" And light appeared. Genesis 1:3 (MSG)

2 GOD MADE BIG MOUNTAINS AND WIDE OCEANS

In this session, the children will:

- find wonder in mountains and oceans
- understand them as made by our great, big God

God makes the biggest and best waves – listen to them roar!" Jeremiah 31:35 (LWC)

3 GOD MADE THINGS THAT GROW

In this session, the children will:

- find wonder in different plants, fruits and flowers
- understand them as wonderfully made by God

The mountains and the hills will shout loud songs – and the trees clap their hands. Isaiah 55:12 (LWC)

4 GOD MADE THE UNIVERSE

In this session, the children will:

- find wonder in the universe
- understand it as made by God

He knows how many stars there are. He gives names to all of them. God is GREAT! Psalm 147:4-5 (LWC)

5 GOD MADE THE FISH AND THE BIRDS

In this session, the children will:

- find wonder in different kinds of fish and birds
- understand them as made by God

God spoke: Swarm, Ocean, with fish and all sea life!
Birds, fly through the sky over Earth! Genesis 1:20 (MSG)

6 GOD MADE AMAZING ANIMALS

In this session, the children will:

- find wonder in different kinds of animals
- understand them as made and loved by God

God spoke... and there it was: wild animals... cattle... every sort of reptile and bug. Genesis 1:24-25 (MSG)

7 GOD MADE ME!

In this session, the children will:

- explore how they are made by God and how they are precious to Him

This is how much God loved the world: He gave his Son... John 3:16 (MSG)

8 BEAUTIFUL WORLD, AMAZING GOD!

In this session, the children will:

- explore how we can see God in what He has made
- praise and worship God for His amazing creation

I look at Your world. It shows me You're awesome and loving. Romans 1:20 (LWC)

WORSHIP SONGS

The following worship songs appear in the **Beautiful World** DVD.

1 *Light of the World*
2 *Spirit Break Out*
3 *Blessed Be Your Name*
4 *So Will I*
5 *Hallelujah*
6 *How Great Thou Art*
7 *Great is Our God*
8 *Maker of All Things*

SINGALONG SONGS

In addition to these worship songs, there are three fantastic, simple singalong songs for you to learn with your children across the eight weeks.

1 *This and That*
2 *Everyday Things*
3 *He's Got the Whole World in His Hands* (found in session 6)

MEMORY VERSE

Each session has a Bible verse attached, which the children might like to learn each week. These have been written into the photocopiable colouring sheets at the end of each session plan.

Younger children, however, might like to learn just one simple verse across the series. We would suggest this verse from Romans 1:

I look at Your world. It shows me You're awesome and loving.

Romans 1:20 (LWC)

1 God made the light

In this session, the children will:

- explore what makes light amazing
- understand it as made by God

Genesis 1:3 (MSG)

God spoke: "Light!" And light appeared.

ICE-BREAKER

Preparation level

zero easy medium

GAME: LIGHT TREASURE HUNT

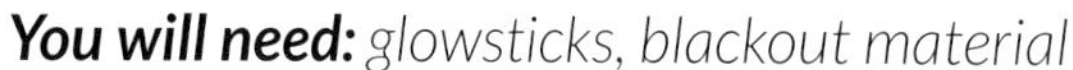

You will need: *glowsticks, blackout material*

For this game to work, your space needs to be dark (but, in the interests of safety, not pitch black). This might require putting blackout materials over the windows if there are no curtains. (Black bin bags work well.)

Before the children come in, hide some glowsticks around the room. As you start the game, turn the lights off. How many glowsticks can they find?

Tip: With small groups, the children could hunt the glowsticks individually. With larger groups, you might want to break the children into smaller teams and run it as a relay – i.e. when one team member finds a glowstick, they bring it back to 'base' and the next team member goes off to search. The fastest team to have every member find a glowstick wins.

LITTLE BIG QUESTION

What's your favourite colour and why?

LITTLE BIG IDEA

ILLUSTRATION: LET THERE BE LIGHT

Explore the different sources of light we find in the world.

With younger children, you might like to show different kinds of lights – either pictures or the real thing. You might look at lighthouses, the sun, fairy lights, etc. Can they name them? Are they big lights or small lights? Where do you find them? What do they do?

With older children, you might like to ask them how many different sources of light they can name (the sun, candles, etc). Ask them to share any facts that they know about light.

LINK TO MESSAGE

Light is really important to us – and it was made by God.

To introduce this session's message, you might like to play *Genesis 1 re-told* from the DVD.

MESSAGE

Tip: you might like to display pictures of light on a board whilst giving the talk.

- We are exploring the beautiful world that God made.
- The Bible says that the very first thing God made was light. Genesis 1:3 says, "God spoke: 'Light!' And light appeared."
- Light is really important to us. Firstly, it helps us to see things. Just imagine what the world would be like if it was always dark!
- Light helps us to grow. Trees, plants and flowers need the light to make them grow, and so do we! The sun's light keeps us healthy, happy and warm.
- Light also gives us all the amazing colours of the world, because light is made up of all the colours of the rainbow.
- Light is amazing – and God gives it to us. Isn't God amazing?

LET'S WORSHIP

Song: *Light of the World*

Singalong: *This and That*

Prayer: **Beautiful World** thank you prayer

LITTLE GROUPS

PRAYER ACROSTIC

You will need: *paper and pens*

As a group, write a prayer themed around light, starting each line with the letters L – I – G – H – T. Use these to praise and thank God.

SESSION PRAYER

WOW, GOD! Thank you for giving us light. Thank you for painting the world in different colours. Thank you that Your light makes me grow big and strong. God, You are amazing! **Amen.**

GET CRAFTY!

Difficulty level

 *suitable for all ages*  *for older children*

Continue to explore light and colour themes with these craft ideas.

1 SUNCATCHER

You will need: *paper plates, sticky-back plastic, yellow tissue paper, string*

Each child will need a paper plate with the centre cut out.

To make the suncatcher, they need to:

- Cover over the middle with sticky-back plastic.
- Stick on small squares of yellow tissue paper.
- Once the plate is full, attach a piece of string to the top to hang it to the window.

Invite the children to put their light catcher on a window at home, thanking God for light when the sun shines through.

2 STAINED-GLASS RAINBOW

You will need: *black card, sticky-back plastic, scissors, coloured tissue paper*

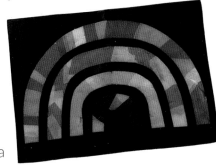

Note: An adult may need to help with some of the cutting stages.

Each child will need a sheet of black card.

To make the stained-glass rainbow:

- Take a black sheet of card and fold it in half.
- Cut from the top of the fold around in a circle to make half a rainbow shape.
- Leave about 2cm and cut a parallel line under the first circle.
- Cut the bottom to join these two cuts. Leave 1cm this time. Cut another parallel line, then another one 2cm away. Again, cut the bottom of these two together.
- Repeat this as many times as necessary or desired, until it looks like a rainbow shape when opened.
- Lay a sheet of sticky-back plastic over the whole piece of card. Lay on different colours of tissue paper to make rainbow colours.

Mount the picture on the window to watch the light shine brightly through your rainbow.

As you make this craft, talk about the beautiful colours we see around us created by the light, and thank God for them.

3 SUNFLOWERS

You will need: *potting soil, sunflower seeds, water, yoghurt pots*

Preparation: Pierce a couple of small holes in the base of the yoghurt pots, to help with draining.

Each child will need one yoghurt pot. To grow the sunflowers:

- Fill the yoghurt pot with soil.
- Plant the seed about 2cm from the top of the soil.
- Water it.
- Place it in a bright space at home and watch the sunflower grow!

(**Note:** Don't overwater the seed, but don't let it dry out. As the sunflower gets bigger, move it into a bigger flowerpot.)

As you plant the seeds, share the amazing creation fact that sunflowers love light and always turn their face towards the sun.

BW1

WOW, GOD!

Little WORSHIP Company

Thank you for giving us light!

2 God made big mountains and wide oceans

In this session, the children will:

- find wonder in mountains and oceans
- understand them as made by our great, big God

Jeremiah 31:35 (LWC)

God makes the biggest and best waves – listen to them roar!

ICE-BREAKER

Preparation level

GAME: SPAGHETTI TOWER

You will need: *packs of spaghetti, marshmallows*

In groups, children have 5 minutes to build the tallest free-standing structure they can manage using spaghetti and marshmallows.

Alternatively, if you have building blocks available, work in groups to see how tall a tower you can build. Use this activity to talk about some of the tallest buildings you've ever seen.

LITTLE BIG QUESTION

Have you ever seen a mountain? When? How did it make you feel?
Have you ever been in the sea? Where? What was it like?

Tip: With younger children, you might like to put pictures of mountains up on a screen. What words describe what they see and how they feel?

LITTLE BIG IDEA

ILLUSTRATION: MAKING WAVES!

You will need: *a large tray, some play sand, lots of water, salt, straws, towels*

Explain to the children that – inspired by Genesis! – you are going to make an ocean. Put the sand at the bottom of the tray for the seabed. Then add the water. (You will need several jugs set up in advance, depending on the size of the tray.) Explain that the seas are salty, so add in some salt. Now, with your ocean set up, it's time to make some waves!

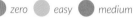

Lay some towels around the edge of the tray to minimise splashes. Invite some children to help you. Ask them to blow air through the straws at the end of the tray to make movement on the water. Invite a few more children to help. Can you get the waves roaring?

LINK TO MESSAGE

The oceans are amazing. And they were made by God!

You might like to show the **session Bible verse**, found on the DVD, here. 

MESSAGE

Tip: You might like to display pictures on a board whilst giving the talk.

- We are looking at how God made the world and everything in it.
- The Bible says that after God made the light, He made the sky, the seas and the land. (Genesis 1:6-10)
- God made wide oceans and big mountains. If you know anything about either of these, you'll know that they are HUGE.
- The world's biggest mountain, Everest, is as tall as 20 skyscrapers stacked on top of each other. That's pretty big!
- But that's nothing compared to the oceans. The world's biggest ocean, the Pacific Ocean, is bigger than ALL the countries of the world put together. It goes so deep, that if Mount Everest sat on the ocean floor, it still wouldn't reach the surface!
- The Bible says that, as big as they are, God is even BIGGER. He made the mountains and the oceans. And He holds them all in His hands. Isn't God amazing?

LET'S WORSHIP

Song: *Spirit Break Out*

Singalong: *This and That*

Prayer: **Beautiful World** thank you prayer

LITTLE GROUPS

OCEAN PRAYERS

You will need: *a big bowl of water – one per group, towels*

Make sure the children are sitting comfortably and can see the bowl. Stir up the water in the bowl so that it makes waves. Let the children watch the waves return to a still place. Talk about what happened to the water.

Explain that sometimes things can happen that will make us feel churned up like the water. But God is big and powerful, and He's with us. He can make us feel peaceful again.

Stir up the water again. Invite the children to think of something that is worrying them, or that they feel anxious about. Let them watch the water return to stillness, knowing that God gives them His peace. Pray for others in the same way. Is there somebody they know who needs God's peace?

SESSION PRAYER

WOW, GOD! Thank you for big mountains and enormous oceans! Thank you that You are bigger than all of them, and that You hold them – and me – in Your hands. **Amen.**

GET CRAFTY!

Continue to explore mountains and oceans with these themed craft ideas.

1 FOAM WAVES

You will need: *a large tray, shaving foam, blue food colouring*

- Find a giant tray or dish and squirt in lashings of shaving foam and some drops of blue food colouring.
- Allow the children to create their own waves from the shaving foam, as they mix the colouring into the foam.

As the children play, invite them to imagine the sea, thanking God for making it.

2 DVD STONE PAINTING

You will need: *stones or shells, paints or colouring pens, other decorating materials (optional)*

Preparation: Gather some stones and seashells when you are next in the park or at the seaside.

Each child will need a stone or a shell to decorate. They could paint faces, pictures, or even add glitter or googly eyes to their designs.

As you decorate these, think about how God made rocks and mountains.

3 MOUNTAIN RANGE COLLAGE

You will need: *coloured craft paper, A4 or A3 paper, chalk (optional)*

Preparation: You will need to cut out different-sized triangles in grey, blue and black. Use the palest colours for the largest triangles.

Each child will need a large piece of paper. To create their collage, they will need to:

- Collect triangles in different colours and sizes.
- Put the biggest triangles down first, then layer the smaller triangles in the foreground.
- Finish the picture by adding white chalk 'snow' to the tops of the triangles.
- You might like to add a Bible verse to the picture: **"The mountain peaks belong to God."** (Psalm 95:4, LWC).

BW2

WOW, GOD!
I praise You for
huge
mountains
and
wide
oceans!
Little
WORSHIP
Company

3 God made things that grow

In this session, the children will:

- find wonder in different plants, fruits and flowers
- understand them as wonderfully made by God

Isaiah 55:12 (LWC)

The mountains and the hills will shout loud songs – and the trees clap their hands.

ICE-BREAKER

Preparation level

GAME: TWO-MINUTE CHALLENGE

You will need: *paper and pens*

Break the children into teams. Set them a two-minute challenge: how many different kinds of vegetables can they name? You may need an adult in the group with the children to help them record their ideas.

You could run other rounds on a similar theme – e.g. name fruit, flowers, or trees.

TIP: If using this with a small group, sit in a circle. Go round the circle, with each person naming something from the starter category, until you run out of ideas.

LITTLE BIG QUESTION

Have you ever grown anything? What was it? What did you need to do? Was it easy or difficult?

LITTLE BIG IDEA

ILLUSTRATION: BIG BOX OF GROWING THINGS

You will need: *different examples of 'growing things', a big box or bag*

Look into your 'big box' to find examples of growing things. Do the children know what they are? Invite them to look/touch/smell/(if appropriate) taste them.

Some suggestions include:

- a bunch of flowers
- potted herbs, e.g. rosemary, sage
- fruits such as strawberries or mangoes
- salad leaves

For older children, you might want to choose more unusual fruits and plants. Talk about which ones the children like the best and why.

LINK TO MESSAGE

Growing things are fantastic! And they were made by God.

You might like to show the **session Bible verse**, found on the DVD, here.

MESSAGE

Tip: You might like to display pictures on a board whilst giving the talk.

- We are looking at how God made the world and everything in it.
- The Bible says that after God made the land, He filled it with all kinds of growing things, from big, tall trees to bright, colourful flowers. (See Genesis 1:11-13.)
- Growing things are amazing. They are beautiful to see and smell. What's more, they provide us with everything we need to live well.
- Most of the food that we get is from plants. We've looked at fruit and vegetables. But flour to make bread, cakes and pasta comes from wheat that's grown in fields. Rice and tea are also grown on plants.
- Wood from trees provides lots of people around the world with shelter.
- Trees and flowers have an important role in making clean air for us to breathe.
- Growing things do so much – and not just for us, but for millions of animals, birds and insects too. The Bible says that God made them and gave them to us. Isn't God amazing?

LET'S WORSHIP

Song: *Blessed Be Your Name*

Singalong: *This and That*

Prayer: **Beautiful World** thank you prayer

LITTLE GROUPS

FRUIT KEBABS

You will need: *different kinds of interesting fruits, chopping board, knife, kebab skewers*

Every group will need one responsible adult to do all the chopping.

In groups, explore the different fruits. Look at the different colours, sizes, shapes, etc. The adult leader 'dissects' the fruit. Think about what the fruit looks like on the inside. Search for the seeds – are there pips or a stone? What does it feel like?

Chop up the fruit. Each child can make their own fruit kebab – to eat then or take away. Thank God as you do so.

SESSION PRAYER

WOW, GOD! Thank you for tall trees and beautiful flowers. Thank you for juicy fruit and tasty vegetables. Thank you that You give us everything that we will ever need. You are so amazing! **Amen.**

GET CRAFTY!

Difficulty level

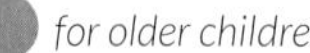

suitable for all ages for older children

Continue to explore growing things with these themed craft ideas.

1 APPLE TREE PRINTING

You will need: *craft paper or card, brown felt tips, apples, red and green paint*

Preparation: Cut the apples in half.

Each child will need a piece of card.

To make the tree:

- Draw a tree trunk on the card.
- Dip a piece of apple in the paint.
- Make prints over the tree.

Don't forget – have a bowl of soapy water and a towel ready to clean little hands!

As you do the craft, talk to the children about the different growing things around them – such as trees and crops – and praise God for them.

2 GRASS SEED YOGHURT POT

You will need: *yoghurt pots, decorating materials, cotton wool, water, grass or cress seeds*

Each child will need a yoghurt pot.

- Decorate the pot with stickers and paints.
- Fill the yoghurt pot with cotton wool.
- Pour some water over to make it damp but not soaking.
- Sprinkle grass or cress seeds onto the cotton wool.
- Take it home and put it in a sunny spot.

Over the coming two weeks the seeds will sprout, showing God's handiwork in action!

3 DVD FLOWER CRAFT

You will need: *tissue paper, pipe cleaners, paper cups, straws*

Each child will need three colours of tissue paper.

To make the flower:

- Layer the pieces of tissue paper on top of each other in long, thick strips.
- Carefully fold them back and forward so they are all pinched together.
- Tightly wrap a pipe cleaner around the middle of the tissue paper.
- Gently unfold the tissue paper so it begins to fluff up into a big ball.
- Push the pipe cleaner through the top of a straw to make the stalk.
- 'Plant' the flower by turning a paper cup upside down and making a small hole in the top to push the flower stalk through.

As you do this craft, ask the children about their favourite kinds of flowers, and praise God for them.

WOW, GOD!
Thank you
for making
things that grow!
Little
WORSHIP
Company
BW3

God made the universe

In this session, the children will:

- find wonder in the universe
- understand it as made by God

Psalm 147:4-5 (LWC)

He knows how many stars there are. He gives names to all of them. God is GREAT!

ICE-BREAKER

Preparation level

zero easy medium

GAME: PASS THE PLANET

You will need: *balls of different sizes e.g. plastic 'play' balls, tennis balls, small footballs; buckets*

Break the children into teams and arrange them into a single line. At the end of the line, place a bucket containing a variety of balls. These are 'planets'. Explain that you are going to assemble a galaxy – with the children's help.

To play the game, each team member must pass the planet along the line to the front, without using their hands. (Under chin, using elbows, between knees, etc is fine.)

When the planet reaches the front, that team member must take it to the leader, who will place it on a table. The group that passes all their planets most quickly wins.

Tip: Depending on the groups' ages, you might want to keep the number of planets per team fairly low.

LITTLE BIG QUESTION:

How many stars are in the universe?

The answer is: nobody knows! There are trillions and trillions – too many to count.

LITTLE BIG IDEA

ILLUSTRATION: SPACE WALK

To prepare for this, create a slide show containing pictures of things you would see in space: e.g. planet Earth, the moon, the sun, stars, other planets, satellites, and asteroids.

Explain that you are going to explore space. Prepare the children for their (imaginary) space journey: put on spacesuit and boots, get into a rocket and blast off. Look at the different things you can see from the spaceship by showing your pictures. Look back at Earth, get to the moon, see stars and asteroids as you pass, etc.

LINK TO MESSAGE

The universe is amazing! And it was made by God.

You might like to show the **session Bible verse**, found on the DVD, here. 

MESSAGE

Tip: you might like to display pictures on a board whilst giving the talk.

- We are looking at how God made the world and everything in it.
- The Bible says that God didn't just make the world. He made things that are out of this world – the sun, moon, stars and planets too. (See Genesis 1:14-19.)
- If you thought the world was big, it's really nothing compared to space! Space is mind-bogglingly huge. We live on planet Earth – which is just one planet in our solar system.
- Planet Earth is like one house on a street called 'the solar system'. And there are lots of solar systems in our galaxy – like there are lots of streets in a town.
- But space is even bigger than this. Just like there are lots of towns in a country, there are lots of galaxies in a universe. That's huge!
- Human beings have been studying space for a long, LONG time. Try as we might, we'll never know all there is to know about our universe. We don't even know how many stars there are – it's impossible to count them all!
- But God knows all about the universe. The Bible says, "He knows how many stars there are. He gives names to all of them." (Psalm 147:4-5). He made the universe and knows every inch of it.
- But there's something even more incredible than this. The God of the universe knows our name too and every part of us. Isn't God amazing?

LET'S WORSHIP

Song: *So Will I*

Singalong: *This and That*

Prayer: **Beautiful World** thank you prayer

LITTLE GROUPS

QUESTION TIME

You will need: *pens and paper (optional)*

Talk about and write up any questions you have about space. Put them on a wonder wall. Read and reflect on them together. Thank God that even if you don't know the answer, He does!

SESSION PRAYER

WOW, GOD! Thank you for the bright sun. Thank you for twinkling stars. Thank you that You know every bit of our universe – and that You know me too. **Amen.**

GET CRAFTY!

Difficulty level
suitable for all ages | for older children

Enjoy making these space-themed crafts as a reminder of the amazing universe God created!

1 UNIVERSE JAR

You will need: *plastic bottles, decorating materials, glitter glue, glitter, food colouring, warm water*

Each child will need their own plastic bottle, representing the 'jar'.

To make the universe jar:

- Fill the jar halfway up with warm water.
- Squirt some glitter glue into the jar (about 50ml of it).
- Add a tiny bit of food colouring gel.
- Screw the lid on and shake it hard.
- Add some glitter and fill the rest up with warm water. (Make sure there is a gap in the top because the jar needs an air bubble.)
- Screw the top on very tightly – the universe jar is complete! Shake it and praise God for His marvellous, mysterious creation.

2 POMPOM STAR SHOOTER

You will need: *paper cups, balloons, craft pompoms, scissors, decorating materials*

Each child will need a paper cup.

To make a pompom star shooter:

- Cut off the bottom of the cup.
- Cut a hole in the top of the balloon, big enough to stretch over the lip on the top of the cup.
- Knot the balloon. (An adult may need to help with this stage!)
- Decorate the cup, e.g. with stickers.

The pompom star shooter is now ready to use. Put a small pompom or craft ball into the cup, pull back the knot in the balloon and PING! Enjoy watching the shooting stars!

3 UNIVERSE MOBILE

You will need: *craft (lollipop) sticks, ribbon, string, craft shapes or stickers (stars, moons, rockets, etc.)*

Each child will need two craft sticks.

To make the mobile:

- Tie the sticks together with ribbon to make a cross shape. (Leave a length of ribbon to hang it up at the end.)
- Attach a piece of string to each end of the sticks (i.e. four lengths of string).
- Attach universe-themed stickers or craft shapes onto each piece of string to make a floating universe.

BW4

Little WORSHIP Company

WOW, GOD!

The universe is AMAZING!

5 God made the fish and the birds

In this session, the children will:

- find wonder in different kinds of fish and birds
- understand them as made by God

Genesis 1:20 (MSG)

**God spoke:
Swarm, Ocean, with fish and all sea life!
Birds, fly through the sky over Earth!**

ICE-BREAKER

Preparation level

 zero easy  medium

GAME: GONE FISHING

You will need: *a big space to play this game*

This is a version of 'tag'. Choose one child to be the person catching fish. Everybody else is a fish.

When the fisherperson catches a fish, the two hold hands. They will catch the next one as a pair. When fish are caught, they join the chain. The chain will get longer as the game goes on. Keep playing until all the fish are caught.

If space is limited, or if you have a smaller group, you could create a simple fishing game with small fish-shaped cards with paper clips attached, and magnetic fishing lines. Put the fish into a deep box – your pond. Blindfold the child fishing. Let them drop the line into the 'pond' and see how many they can draw out. Give everybody a turn. Who managed to get the most?

LITTLE BIG QUESTION

Would you rather be a fish or a bird? Why?

LITTLE BIG IDEA

ILLUSTRATION: FISH OR BIRD

Create a slide show of different birds and fish to share with the children. Use it to inspire wonder in God's amazing creation.

For younger children, you might like to compile a range of different birds and sea creatures and ask them if they can identify them. You could include:

- **birds –** ostrich, penguin, robin, parrot, owl, pigeon, eagle, peacock
- **sea creatures –** dolphin, octopus, clownfish, starfish, sea horse, crab, jellyfish

For older children, you might like to play a round of **'fish or bird?'** Create a slide show with a range of species names from across the sky and sea. Can they guess if it's a fish or a bird? Play as individuals or in teams. When the children have voted, reveal the picture answer.

Suggestions:

- cassowary (bird)
- tropical gnatcatcher (bird)
- dragon goby (fish)
- flagtail (fish)
- water ouzel (bird – also known as the American Dipper)
- mahi-mahi (fish)
- yellowhammer (bird)
- tiger perch (fish)
- wahoo (fish)
- black-spotted bare-eye (bird)

LINK TO MESSAGE

Fish and birds are amazing! And God made all of them.

To introduce this session's message, you might like to show *Things in the sea* from the DVD.

MESSAGE

Tip: you might like to display pictures on a board whilst giving the talk.

- We are looking at how God made the world and everything in it.
- The Bible says that God saw the skies and the oceans He had made and that He then created all kinds of amazing creatures to live in them. (See Genesis 1:20.)
- He filled the oceans with all kinds of sea creatures – wobbly jellyfish, clever octopuses, graceful dolphins, mighty whales, and many more!
- He filled the sky with birds of all shapes, sizes and colours – from little sparrows in the back garden to bright parrots in the rainforests.
- There are millions of birds and fish all over our planet. It's actually impossible to know exactly how many there are.
- The oceans go so deep and wide that nobody has yet managed to explore them to find all the fish. The jungles are so dense that it's impossible to count all the birds that live in their trees.
- There are all kinds of incredible creatures on our planet that we still know nothing about. But God made them all, and He knows them all. Isn't God amazing?

LET'S WORSHIP

Song: *Hallelujah*

Singalong: *Everyday Things*

Prayer: **Beautiful World** thank you prayer

LITTLE GROUPS

JUNK MODEL CREATION

You will need: *junk model materials or pens and paper*

In groups, talk about some of the most interesting birds or fish you have seen.

Let the children design their own bird or fish. Where does it live? What can it do?

Do this individually or as a group. Use a big sheet of paper, or 'junk model' it as a craft. As you do, praise God for His amazing creations.

SESSION PRAYER

WOW, GOD! Thank you for weird and wonderful fish in the sea. Thank you for bright birds with beautiful voices. Thank you for everything that You've made! **Amen.**

GET CRAFTY!

Difficulty level

suitable for all ages *for older children*

God made all kinds of incredible fish and birds! Let the children have a go at making their own. Alternatively, help them to look after God's creation with their own bird feeder.

1 PAPER PLATE FISH 

You will need: *paper plates, glue, scissors, googly eyes, tissue paper cut into squares*

To make a paper plate fish:

- Cut a triangle like a pizza slice out of a paper plate.
- Stick this triangle onto the other side of the plate as a tail.
- Decorate with tissue paper and googly eyes to finish.

2 PAPER PLATE BIRD

You will need: *paper plates, googly eyes, feathers, tissue paper, glue, scissors, coloured paper, sticky tape*

Preparation: You might like to cut small yellow triangles in advance, to make the bird's beak.

To make a paper plate bird:

- Fold a paper plate in half.
- Attach a paper beak and a googly eye to one side.
- Stick craft feathers to its side and a collection of brightly-coloured tissue streamers to make up its tail.
- Join these to the back of the bird using tape.

3 PINE CONE BIRD FEEDER 

You will need: *a pine cone, some ribbon, some birdseed, blocks of baking butter*

To make the bird feeder:

- Tie a ribbon around the top of the pine cone (to hang it on a branch).
- Squish the baking butter into the pine cone using your hands.
- Roll the stuffed pine cone in birdseed.
- Take it home and hang it in the garden.

WOW, GOD!

Little WORSHIP Company

Thank you for making fish in the sea and birds in the air.

BW5

6 God made amazing animals

In this session, the children will:

- find wonder in different kinds of animals
- understand them as made and loved by God

Genesis 1:24-25 (MSG)

God spoke... and there it was: wild animals... cattle... every sort of reptile and bug.

ICE-BREAKER

GAME: ANIMAL CHARADES

You will need: *different animal names written on pieces of paper and put in a 'hat' (suggestions: dog, caterpillar, snake, frog, horse, elephant, lion, cat)*

Play this game as one big group, or in smaller groups. One person takes an animal from the hat and mimes it to the others for them to guess. Allow sounds if really necessary!

LITTLE BIG QUESTION

If you could have any animal for a pet, what would it be and why?

LITTLE BIG IDEA

ILLUSTRATION: AMAZING ANIMALS!

Create a slide show of different amazing animals to share with the children. Use it to inspire wonder in God's amazing creation.

For younger children, look at 10 different animals or creepy-crawlies. Can they identify them? Have they ever seen any themselves? Where?

For older children, you might like to explore some of the world's most 'amazing animals' by running our quiz (see appendix). Make the quiz more active by asking children to move to different corners of the room when choosing their answer.

Alternatively, for this session you might like to bring in an animal to show the children, subject to suitable risk assessment.

LINK TO MESSAGE

Animals are amazing! And God made and loves them all.

To introduce this session's message, you might like to play the song *He's Got the Whole World in His Hands* from the DVD.

MESSAGE

Tip: you might like to display pictures on a board whilst giving the talk.

- We are looking at how God made the world and everything in it.
- The Bible says that God filled the world with all kinds of amazing animals (see Genesis 1:24-25). God made big ones, small ones, fluffy ones and fierce ones.
- He also made all kinds of insects that live in the trees and soil, as well as reptiles like snakes and lizards.
- Animals have been good friends to humans for many years – from being loving pets, to helping with farming, to providing us with milk to drink.
- Lots of insects do incredible jobs for the good of the planet every day. Even little creatures like ants, bees and worms do big things for us, keeping the soil clean and helping the plants to grow.
- There are literally millions of different kinds of animals and insects on our planet – and that includes some we've not even discovered yet.
- But God made them, knows them and loves all of them. Isn't God amazing?

LET'S WORSHIP

Song: *How Great Thou Art*

Singalong: *Everyday Things*

Prayer: **Beautiful World** thank you prayer

LITTLE GROUPS

ALL THINGS WEIRD AND WONDERFUL...

You will need: *big paper, pens*

Give the children some paper and pens. Can they design a new weird and wonderful animal using different parts of existing animals, e.g. a giraffe's neck, an elephant's trunk, etc? Do this individually or as a group.

Create your own group art gallery to display your wonderful creations – and thank God for His!

SESSION PRAYER

WOW, GOD! Thank you for amazing animals and creepy-crawlies. Thank you for things that run and things that wriggle. Thank you for everything You've made! **Amen.**

GET CRAFTY!

Difficulty level

suitable for all ages  for older children

God made all kinds of amazing animals and creepy-crawlies. Let the children have a go at sculpting a few of their own.

1 MODELLING CLAY HEDGEHOG

You will need: *play dough (find a recipe in the* ***Amazing Me*** *appendix), spaghetti, googly eyes (optional)*

Each child will need some play dough in a round ball.

To make the hedgehog:

- Squash the end to make a nose.
- Make some eyes with a pencil or attach some googly eyes.
- Make the hedgehog's spikes by pushing little pieces of spaghetti into the play dough.

2 CATERPILLAR PAPER CHAIN

You will need: *strips of coloured paper, sticky tape or glue, pipe cleaner, googly eyes (optional)*

To make the caterpillar:

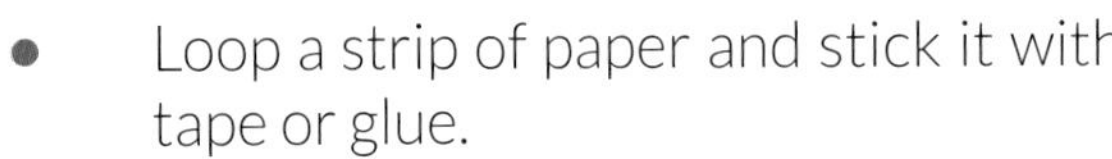

- Loop a strip of paper and stick it with tape or glue.

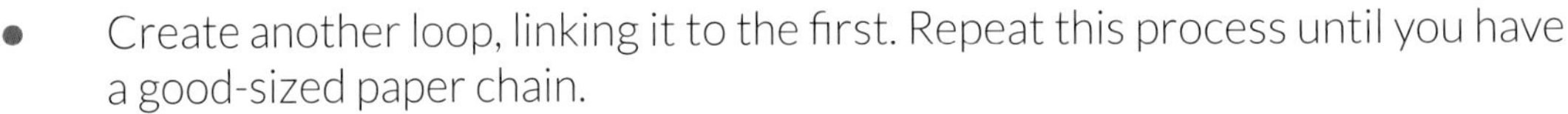

- Create another loop, linking it to the first. Repeat this process until you have a good-sized paper chain.
- For the head, draw a face on the paper before looping and sticking it.
- Add some pipe cleaner antennae and googly eyes for effect.

3 INSECT MODELLING

You will need: *assorted junk and craft items e.g. toilet rolls, pipe cleaners, tissue paper, googly eyes, pens*

Let the children make their own insects out of the materials provided. You might like to provide a few pictures of different insects for inspiration.

BW6

WOW, GOD!

Thank you for making amazing animals!

Little WORSHIP Company

God made ME!

In this session, the children will:

- explore how they are made by God and precious to Him.

John 3:16 (MSG)

This is how much God loved the world: He gave his Son...

ICE-BREAKER

Preparation level

GAME: MARVELLOUS ME

You will need: *a parachute*

Stand the children in a circle holding the parachute. Practise lifting it up and lowering it together.

To run the game, get the children to shake and lift the parachute. Call out a feature – for example, brown eyes. Anybody who has brown eyes needs to let go of the parachute, run into the middle and out again to a new place in the circle.

Use different personal features that the children can easily identify with – for example, hair or eye colour, favourite hobbies, birthday month, etc.

Tip: This can be run without a parachute. Sit the children in a circle. When you call out a feature, whoever it applies to needs to jump up and swap places with somebody else.

LITTLE BIG QUESTION

What's the greatest thing you have ever made?

LITTLE BIG IDEA

ILLUSTRATION: CREATION BOX

You will need: *a big box, items representing the different stages of creation (e.g. a torch representing light, some play animals, pebbles for the mountains, etc), a medium-sized mirror*

Introduce the children to your 'creation box'. Inside are all the different things God made.

See how many the children can remember from previous weeks. As they name them, bring the relevant items out of the box and display them.

Explain that there's one last thing that God made after all the rest – and it's in the box. Build up the anticipation by looking into the box with wonder and amazement. This last thing is the best by far. You've never seen anything so incredible! Do the children want to see what it is?

When they can't wait any longer, bring out a mirror and point it towards the children. The last, most wonderful thing God made was... them!

LINK TO MESSAGE

Every single one of us is made and loved by God too. We are His amazing creation.

To introduce this session's message, you might like to play *How much does God love you?* from the DVD.

MESSAGE

- We have been looking at how God made the world and everything in it.
- The Bible says that He made the light, sea, sky, land, universe, fish, birds and animals. And He saw that all of it was good.
- Then God made one last thing. He made people. And He thought we were very good. (See Genesis 1:26-27;31.)
- The Bible says that we are really, really special to God. God made us to be His friends. He knows us and He loves us more than we can ever imagine.
- The Bible says, "This is how much God loved the world: He gave his Son..." (John 3:16) In other words, God who made the universe loves us so much that He became a tiny human. He was born as a baby called Jesus. He came to live with us so that we could know Him better.
- When Jesus died, he made a special way for us to be friends with God forever. That means that we can know God and be friends with Him today.
- God's love for us is BIGGER than the huge universe He created. Isn't God amazing?

LET'S WORSHIP

Song: *Great is Our God*
Singalong: *Everyday Things*
Prayer: **Beautiful World** thank you prayer

LITTLE GROUPS

PRAY DOUGH

You will need: *some play dough (a recipe can be found in the* ***Amazing Me*** *appendix)*

Invite the children to create themselves out of play dough. Talk about the things which make each of them unique. Encourage them to think about God making them: how He made them with different talents, personalities and interests, and how He loves them completely.

When the children have finished, thank God for His marvellous creations.

SESSION PRAYER

WOW, GOD! Thank you that You made me. Thank you that You love me. Thank you that, even though You are really, really BIG, You made Yourself into a teeny tiny person so that I could be Your friend forever. **Amen.**

GET CRAFTY!

Difficulty level
suitable for all ages | for older children

Continue exploring how God made us and loves us with these themed craft ideas.

1 EDIBLE FACE

You will need: *tortilla wraps, various healthy ingredients*

To make an edible face:

- Use a wrap for a face.
- Make the features out of grapes, raisins, cucumber, peppers, etc.
- You could make hair from carrots that have been spiralized. Alternatively, use grated cheese.

2 MIRROR

You will need: *scissors, sticky tape, card, foil, craft (lollipop) sticks, decorating materials*

Each child will need one piece of card and some foil.

To make the mirror:

- Fold the card in half and draw a circle or an oval on one side.
- Cut out the circle. (An adult will need to help younger children with this step.)
- On the other side of the card, stick a piece of foil and a craft stick, so that the foil can be seen through the hole when the card is folded together.
- Stick it shut and decorate the front with jewelled stickers, glitter, etc.

Invite the children to look in the mirror, remembering not just how God made them, but how much He loves them too.

3 DVD PEG DOLL FAMILY

You will need: *old-fashioned wooden pegs (i.e. not hinged), felt tips, paints, pieces of fabric*

Each child will need a peg.

To decorate the peg doll:

- Colour the hair using either pens or paints.
- Draw eyes, nose and mouth with a black pen.
- Paint some clothes on or create clothes out of pieces of fabric.

Assemble the children's peg dolls together, thinking about how God made and loves everyone in the world!

BW7

This is how much God loved the world: He gave his Son...

Little WORSHIP Company

John 3:16
MSG

8 Beautiful world, amazing God!

In this session, the children will:

- explore how we can see God in what He has made
- praise and worship God for His amazing creation

Romans 1:20 (LWC)

I look at Your world.
It shows me You're awesome and loving!

ICE-BREAKER

Preparation level: zero, easy, medium

GAME: CREATION WARM-UP

You will need: *music*

Before you begin, learn some creation dance moves/actions.

- Light – spin around like a lighthouse
- Mountains – arms overhead, joined together
- Oceans – spin arms backwards, as though doing backstroke
- Trees – raise arms and sway side to side
- Stars – jump up, stretch out arms and make a big 'explosion' noise
- Fish – wriggle your arms and legs like an octopus
- Birds – soar around the room with arms outstretched
- Animals – freestyle your favourite animal!
- People – shake hands with somebody nearby

Play some music. Call out the different creation dance moves for the children to join in with until the music ends.

Tip: You could do this without music. The children could walk around, doing the different actions as you call them. Make it a game by making the last person to respond 'out'.

LITTLE BIG QUESTION:

What's the most amazing thing in the world? (You might like to think about some of the different things you've explored over previous weeks!)

LITTLE BIG IDEA

ILLUSTRATION: JIGSAWS

Preparation: Draw a big picture across 9 sheets of A4 paper in a 3x3 formation. Choose something simple – e.g. a picture of a house or a tree.

Talk about your wonderful piece of art that you are going to put together. Assemble the picture one piece at a time. (Try not to use adjoining pieces to sustain the mystery!) Can the children guess what you are making?

With older children, you might like to run a jigsaw race instead. Break the children into teams or choose a few volunteers. Give out one jigsaw per group/child. Who can assemble it the fastest?

LINK TO MESSAGE

The different pieces of a jigsaw come together to make one big picture. And the different bits of creation are like a jigsaw too – coming together to show us one big, AMAZING God!

You might like to show the **session Bible verse**, found on the DVD, here. 

MESSAGE

- We live in an incredible world. There's so much to make you say 'wow'. Mountains, oceans, stars, fish, birds and animals – plus you and me!
- The Bible says that God made this wonderful world. In the New Testament, one of God's special friends, Paul, said: "I look at Your world. It shows me You're awesome and loving." (Romans 1:20). In other words, when we look around us, we can get an idea of what God Himself is like.
- Creation (i.e. all that God has made) shows us how BIG God is. Just think of the size of it – the mountains, oceans, and stars in the sky. And God is even bigger!
- Creation shows us that God has an amazing imagination. Just look at all the incredible birds, fish, animals and insects He's made!
- More than anything, creation shows us just how much God loves us. He has given us everything we need to live happily and healthily – not just food, clothes and shelter, but love too: from family and friends and from God Himself.
- We live in an amazing world. But the God who made it is even MORE amazing. So next time you see something that makes you say 'WOW', turn it into worship by praising God and saying 'thank you' for it.
- What a beautiful world. And what an AWESOME God!

LET'S WORSHIP

Song: *Maker of All Things*

Singalong: *Everyday Things*

Prayer: **Beautiful World** thank you prayer

LITTLE GROUPS

PRAISE BALL

You will need: *a large, soft ball*

Sit together in a large circle on the floor. Pass the ball to each other.

Whoever catches the ball needs to say something they find amazing in creation – for example, "Thank you, God, for starry skies." It can be anything – from something huge and impressive to something tiny that they are simply thankful for.

SESSION PRAYER

WOW, GOD! You are AMAZING! Thank you for the beautiful world that You made. Thank you that You love and care for everything in it – including me. I love You, God! **Amen.**

GET CRAFTY!

Difficulty level

suitable for all ages

for older children

Think about God's beautiful world with these creation-themed crafts.

1 CREATION BISCUITS

You will need: *ready-made puff pastry, grated cheese, herbs (optional), a blunt knife or 'creation' cutters (flowers, stars, animals, people, etc.)*

To make the biscuits:

- Lay out the ready-rolled puff pastry.
- Cut out shapes with a blunt knife or some cutters.
- Lay them on a baking tray and put grated cheese over them.
- Add some dried herbs for additional flavour.
- Bake according to the instructions on the pastry packet and enjoy eating them together.

2 CREATION GARDEN

You will need: *shallow trays, pebbles, green felt or moss, plastic lids, water, artificial flowers, miniature toy animals*

Each child will need their own tray.

To make a beautiful garden of Eden:

- Put the green felt or moss down to make grass.
- Add pebbles to provide some extra texture.
- Put in a plastic lid and fill it with water to make a pond.
- Add in a few little animals or birds and some artificial flowers.

Tip: You could use real soil as a base, sprinkle some grass seed, water it and watch it grow into a real garden.

3 COLOURFUL BRACELET

You will need: *pipe cleaners, colourful beads*

To make the bracelet:

- Thread the beads onto the pipe cleaner.
- When finished, tie the ends around your wrist.

As the children wear their own beautiful creation, invite them to remember God's beautiful creation and say thank you for it.

BW8

I look at the world and it shows me You are awesome!

Romans 1:20
LWC

Little WORSHIP Company

BEAUTIFUL WORLD
All-age worship

At the end of the curriculum course, you may like to lead a Sunday morning, all-age worship service on the curriculum's theme, inviting the children to participate in leading it.

Follow or adapt the service plan below as appropriate for your congregation.

WELCOME

Welcome the congregation to the service.

OPENING PRAYER

Dear God, we're so excited to meet together [this morning] to explore your beautiful world. As we look at all the wonderful things You have made – from the seas to the stars, from little ants to enormous elephants – help us to see more of You, the even-more-wonderful God who made everything. **Amen.**

WORSHIP

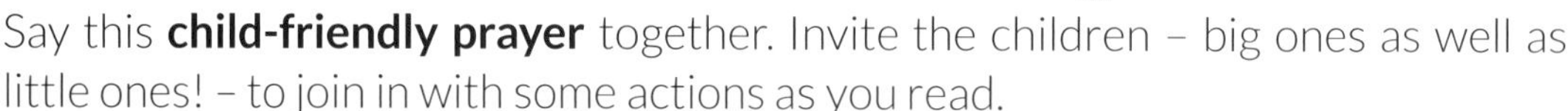

Sing a couple of **songs** from the **Beautiful World** DVD.

Say this **child-friendly prayer** together. Invite the children – big ones as well as little ones! – to join in with some actions as you read.

ALL-AGE LITURGY

Thank you, God, for Your whole world.

Thank you for windy rivers.

Thank you for tall mountains.

Thank you for green trees.

Thank you for blue seas.

Thank you for beautiful flowers.

Thank you for all the creatures.

Thank you for starry nights.

Thank you for my family… and for me!

Thank you, God, that You have the whole world in Your hands.

Amen.

CHILDREN'S SLOT

Invite the children to the front to talk about the different things they have learnt over the last few weeks. They might like to share some of the crafts they have made, or any memory verses they have learnt.

The children may also like to sing a **Beautiful World singalong song.** 
Perhaps they could teach it to the adults!

WORD

Read one or more of the suggested **Bible readings** (or choose your own). Invite a range of readers – young and old – to do this.

- **Genesis 1:26 to 2:1** The conclusion of the creation account in Genesis 1, when God made us to live in His amazing world.
- **Psalm 8** Praising God for His marvellous creation and awesome love for us.
- **Revelation 21:1-7** A vision of God's re-creation – the new heaven and new earth, where we live at peace with God and each other.

MESSAGE

Share the suggested message below or create your own.

Key Bible passage: Genesis 1:26-2:1

Key message: God's beautiful world shows us an awesome, good and loving God.

INTRODUCTION

- Inspire wonder in the beautiful world God made. You might choose to do one or more of the following:
    - Show an especially awe-inspiring clip from a nature programme.
    - Show some nature/creation pictures. Turn them into a quiz with the congregation – can they name these wonderful things God has made? (You could tie this in with exploring the creation account by asking if people can name the day on which God made them, according to Genesis.)
- Ask people about their favourite things in creation (i.e. what and why?).
- Ask people if they know any interesting creation-themed facts they would like to share – and/or share some yourself.

REFLECTION

- Over the last few weeks the children have been exploring the **Beautiful World** that God made. Romans 1:20 says:
  "Since the creation of the world God's invisible qualities – his eternal power and divine nature – have been clearly seen, being understood from what has been made."
  In other words, Paul is saying that we can see something of God from this beautiful world He created. So what can we learn about what God is like, as we explore His creation?
- We can see how **big** and **awesome** God is. Just look at the big mountains, the enormous oceans and the vast universe around us. They are huge – and the God who made them is even more magnificent, majestic and mighty, holding them all in His hands.
- We can also see how **good** He is. Look at the trees and plants. God made them, programming them to reproduce each year so that there would be food and shelter for all of us. They show us just how generous God is to all He has made.

- But more than this, we can see how **loving** God is. Genesis makes it clear that God did not make an amazing world and then vanish once it was made. God's plan was always to live **with** us in the world He created – as our friend and Heavenly Father.
- In fact, the big story of the Bible is how much God loves the people He made – even when they forget or ignore Him. He comes to live with them in the person of Jesus. When Jesus died, God made a way to live with all of us by His Spirit so that we can walk with Him today. And the last words of the Bible show God coming to live with His people again in a new heaven and new earth – this time, for all eternity.

PRAYERS

LIGHT IN THE DARKNESS

God made a beautiful world – but it is not currently a perfect one. Use this creation-themed response as a way of praying for light in dark situations.

You will need: *LED candles, glowsticks*

- Give out LED candles to the adults and glowsticks to the children.
- Reflect on the words of Genesis 1:1-3. Reflect on how God brings light into the darkness.
- Think about how we often call hopeless or difficult situations 'dark times'. In these moments, we can turn to God and trust Him to bring light into our darkness too.
- Lead some prayers of intercession. Take a moment to be silent. Invite the congregation to bring a situation to God. It might be a personal matter or something of national or global significance.
- Speak the words of Genesis 1:3: "And God said, 'Let there be light' – and there was light." After you say this, invite the congregation to turn their lights on as a response to the prayer.
- Conclude by saying that Jesus calls us the light of the world. As people wear or look at their lights, pray that God will show them how they might bring hope to those around them this week.

PLANTING PRAYERS

Use this creation-themed activity as an encouraging way to pray.

You will need: *biodegradable pots, a range of seeds, compost*

Preparation: Put potting compost into the pots in advance, to save on mess. Put seeds in little bowls. Put the pre-filled pots and seeds on a couple of stations around the church.

- Reflect on what creation reveals about God: about His power, His provision, and His love.
- Invite the congregation to go to a planting station around the church. Explain that there are different kinds of seeds. Invite them to plant a seed as a prayer.
    - They might choose to plant a **flower seed** for a situation in which they need hope or healing.

- They might plant a **vegetable plant seed** if praying for God's provision.

- Encourage the congregation to keep praying that prayer as they nurture the plant at home, trusting in the God of creation's faithful promises to us.

WORSHIP

Sing one or two **songs** from the **Beautiful World** DVD. (You may like to take up an offering here and/or say the Lord's Prayer together.)

BLESSING AND DISMISSAL

Formally close the service.

CLOSING BLESSING

May the God of light shine on us.
May the God of water refresh us.
May the God of growing things provide for us,
as we who are made in His image share His goodness with those around us.
Amen.

AMAZING ANIMALS QUIZ

Below are some incredible facts about some of God's amazing creatures.

Run the quiz, inviting the children to vote on their answers so that everybody participates. You could ask them to move to different corners of the room. Alternatively, you could give everybody a 'vote ball' and provide 3 buckets labelled A, B and C. After hearing the different multiple-choice answers, the children simply drop their ball into the relevant bucket to indicate their answer.

As you reveal the answer, take some time to dwell on how wonderful and amazing the creatures are – and how wonderful and amazing God is for making them!

QUESTIONS

1 The fastest creature in the world is the cheetah.
But how quickly does it run? Up to 40mph, up to 60mph or up to 75mph?
***[Answer: 75mph.** This means that if it ran along the hard shoulder on the motorway, it would be faster than your car!]*

2 Lions can roar very loudly.
But how far away can you hear them? 6km, 8km or 10km?
***[Answer: 8km.** Provide a local example for how far away that is for you!]*

3 The biggest land animal is the African Elephant.
But how many hours a day does it spend eating? 4 hours, 10 hours or 16 hours?
***[Answer: 16 hours.** That's a lot of food.*
And it drinks between 100 and 200 litres of water a day.]

4 The tropical stick insect is the world's longest insect.
But how long is it? Is it 25cm, 35cm or 45cm?
***[Answer: 35cm.** Take out a ruler to show the children how long that is.*
You might like to get a picture of it on a screen. Imagine meeting that creepy-crawly!]

5 How many times does the honeybee flap its wings in a second?
10 times, 100 times or 200 times?
***[Answer: 200 times.** Use a watch or the stopwatch on your phone to time seconds – that's unbelievably fast!]*

Praise Party
Bible curriculum

PRAISE PARTY

Everyone loves a party – and the best ones of all are praise parties! **Praise Party** helps children to understand what it means to praise and worship God, not only with singing, dancing and instruments, but with their hearts, feet and hands too.

1 PRAISE GOD WITH HEART, MIND, SOUL AND STRENGTH

In this session, the children will:

- explore what we mean by 'praise'
- understand that we love God because He loves us

Love the Lord your God with all your heart, with all your soul, with all your mind and with all your strength. Luke 10:27

2 PRAISE GOD WITH HAPPY SONGS

In this session, the children will:

- explore praising God by singing and dancing to Him

Sing to the Lord a new song; everybody sing to the Lord! Psalm 96:1 (LWC)

3 PRAISE GOD WITH LOUD INSTRUMENTS

In this session, the children will:

- explore praising God by making music to Him

Praise God – He is so great! Praise Him with the loud trumpet. Praise Him with guitars and violins. Praise Him with drums and whistles. Praise Him with tambourines and maracas! Based on Psalm 150:3-5 (LWC)

4 PRAISE GOD WITH GREAT BIG THANK YOUS!

In this session, the children will:

- explore praising God by saying thank you to Him

Say a great big THANK YOU to God! He is so good to us! His love never, EVER runs out! Psalm 136:1 (LWC)

5 PRAISE GOD WITH FOLLOWING FOOTSTEPS

In this session, the children will:

- explore the idea of a 'life of worship' – praising God by what we do as well as what we say
- understand that we can praise God by following Jesus' commands and example

See what God does, and then go and do it yourself! Ephesians 5:1 (LWC)

6 PRAISE GOD WITH HELPFUL HANDS

In this session, the children will:

- explore the story of the Good Samaritan
- understand that we praise God by showing His love to other people

Always love one another. Be joyful and faithful and patient. Share with people in need. Practise being kind. Romans 12:10-13 (LWC)

7 PRAISE GOD WITH ALL OF MY FRIENDS

In this session, the children will:

- explore what happens at church on a Sunday
- understand church as a place to praise God with others

There is a time for everything. A time to play, a time to sleep, a time to read, a time to bounce, a time to eat and a time to party! (LWC, inspired by Ecclesiastes 3)

8 PRAISE GOD WITH EVERYTHING I'VE GOT!

In this session, the children will:

- enjoy a big praise party!

I'm gonna praise God my whole life long! I'll sing to God for as long as I'm alive! Psalm 146:2 (LWC)

WORSHIP SONGS

The following worship songs appear in the **Praise Party** DVD.

1 *Every Move I Make*
2 *Sing to the Lord*
3 *Shake-a-hallelujah*
4 *Happy Day*
5 *Joyful Joyful*
6 *Because of Your Love*
7 *Celebrate*
8 *Dance Dance*

SINGALONG SONGS

In addition to these worship songs, there are two fantastic, simple singalong songs for you to learn with your children across the eight weeks.

1 *Joy*
2 *He's Got the Whole World in His Hands*

MEMORY VERSE

Each session has a Bible verse attached, which the children might like to learn each week. These have been written into the photocopiable colouring sheets at the end of each session plan.

Younger children, however, might like to learn just one simple verse across the series. We would suggest this verse from Psalm 146:

I'm gonna praise God my whole life long! I'll sing to God for as long as I'm alive! Psalm 146:2 (LWC)

1 Praise God with heart, mind, soul and strength

In this session, the children will:

- explore what we mean by 'praise'
- understand that we love God because He loves us

Luke 10:27

Love the Lord your God with all your heart, with all your soul, with all your mind and with all your strength.

ICE-BREAKER

Preparation level

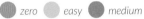

GAME: HEART, MIND, SOUL AND STRENGTH

To play the game, you will need a large, clear space.

This is a version of the classic game 'fruit salad', which should help the children to become familiar with this session's Bible verse.

Sit the children in a circle. Go around the circle, labelling each child either 'heart', 'soul', 'mind' or 'strength'.

Call out (for example), "I'll praise God with my... heart!" Those who were labelled 'heart' jump up and swap places with each other, finding a new place in the circle. Then continue, calling out different ones each time.

Every now and again, call out, "I'll praise God with my heart, soul, mind and strength!" – and enjoy the ensuing chaos!

Tip: If you have only a small number of children, label different corners of the room 'heart', 'soul', 'mind' and 'strength'. Play some music and invite the children to dance along. When the music stops, call out (for example), "Heart!" The children then need to race to the 'heart' corner of the room. Repeat the process using different ones each time.

LITTLE BIG QUESTION

What or whom do you love best?

LITTLE BIG IDEA

ILLUSTRATION: THE LOVE MACHINE

You will need: *a large cardboard box, and various 'love' gift items – e.g. chocolates, a bunch of flowers, a nice card*

Preparation: Draw buttons (e.g. number/letter keys, big buttons) over your cardboard box to make it look like a 'machine'.

Talk to the children about the different people we love.

Explain that you want to show the people that you love just how special they are. Choose one person. Tell the children:

- what they're like and what makes them so special to you
- what they do for you that you're thankful for

Explain that you will program this key information into the machine, and that it will produce something that will help you to show that person how much you love them.

Produce something relevant from the box – e.g. a lovely bunch of flowers which is as beautiful as they are.

Repeat the process a couple of times with different people/gifts.

LINK TO MESSAGE

Presents and cards are one way of showing people the love we feel for them. Praise is our way of showing God all the love we have for Him.

You might like to show the **session Bible verse**, found on the DVD, here. 

MESSAGE

- We are going to be thinking about 'praise'. But what is praise?
- Praise is simply letting God know how wonderful He is and how much we love Him.
- When we think about the people we love, we can usually explain why we love them. It might be because of the things they do for us. It might be because being with them makes us feel happy or peaceful.
- We find ways to show them how special they are to us – in the things we say and the things we do.
- The Bible tells us about how special God is and how much He loves us. He gives us everything that we need every day – and more besides. He promises to always be with us and to help us.
- God loves us more than we can ever imagine. The Bible tells us to love God in return - with our 'heart, mind, soul and strength' (Luke 10:27).
- Giving God praise is our way of showing Him that we love Him and are thankful for all He does. There are lots and lots of different ways to praise and worship God – and we will explore these over the coming weeks. Can you think of any already?

LET'S WORSHIP

Song: *Every Move I Make*

Singalong: *Joy*

Prayer: **Praise Party** thank you prayer

LITTLE GROUPS

HOKEY-COKEY PRAISE 

You will need: *scrap paper, pens*

In groups, invite the children to think of things they want to praise God for.

It might be a statement about what God is like – e.g. God is good. It might be something they are thankful for. Ask them to write any ideas down on a piece of scrap paper. After a couple of minutes, collect up the ideas.

Invite all the children to stand in a big circle and hold hands. Run into the middle, hokey-cokey style. When everybody's in the middle, call out something to praise God for from the children's ideas. As the children come out again, everybody shouts in response, "Thank you, God!"

SESSION PRAYER

Dear God, thank you that You love us more than we can ever imagine. Help us to love You too, with every part of us. **Amen.**

GET CRAFTY!

Difficulty level

Introduce the 'praise' theme by making some of these praise props. Help the children to remember that praise begins in the heart with our potato stamp picture.

1 PRAISE RIBBON

You will need: *a long stick or dowel, ribbons, sticky tape, pipe cleaners, bells and beads (optional)*

To make the praise ribbon:

- Cut several 50cm lengths of colourful ribbons and lay them against the dowel.
- Tape the middle of the ribbon to the top of the dowel, then fold the ribbon in half up over the tape, and tape again.
- Optional: thread bells and beads through some pipe cleaners and wrap them around the dowel.

2  PRAISE WAVER

You will need: *paper plates, ribbons, pipe cleaners, bells and beads (optional)*

Preparation: With younger children, you might like to cut out the inside of the paper plate in advance.

Each child will need a paper plate.

To make your praise waver:

- Cut the centre out of the paper plate.
- Decorate it with colourful ribbons by looping them around the plate.
- **Optional:** thread bells and beads through pipe cleaners and attach them to the praise waver.

3 POTATO HEART STAMPS

You will need: *potatoes, knife or heart-shaped cookie cutter, paints, craft paper*

Preparation: Create heart stamps by cutting a large potato in half. Cut a heart shape into it or push a cookie cutter into the top and trim around the edge.

Let the children dip the potato into a tray of paint and print onto a piece of paper. Older children might like to write the words of Luke 10:27 onto the different heart marks.

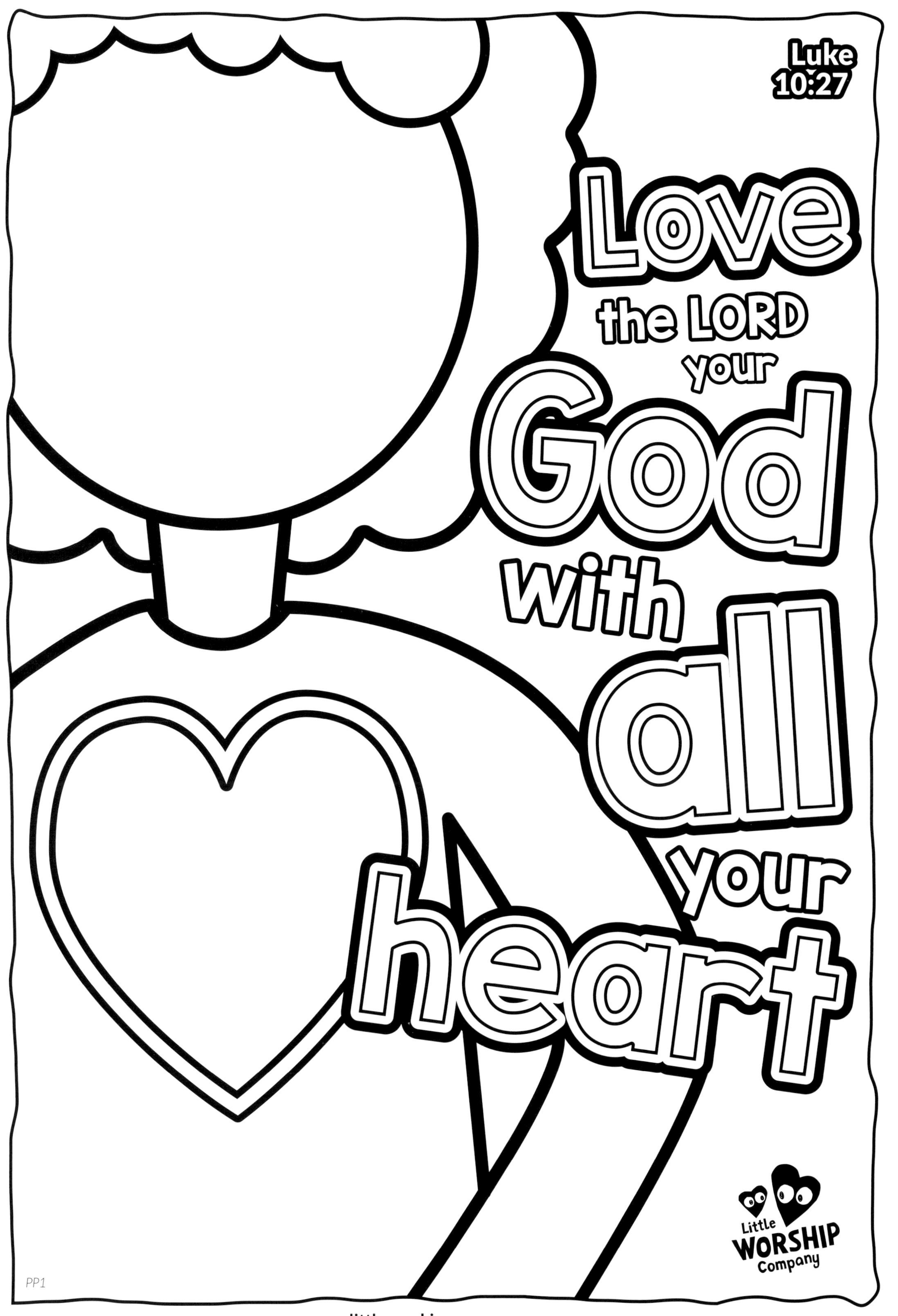
Luke 10:27
Love the LORD your God with all your heart
Little WORSHIP Company

2 Praise God with happy songs

In this session, the children will:

- explore praising God by singing and dancing to Him

Psalm 96:1 (LWC)

Sing to the Lord a new song; everybody sing to the Lord!

ICE-BREAKER

GAME: KAZOO THAT TUNE

You will need: *one or more kazoos, paper and pens*

Preparation: Think of 5–10 well-known TV themes, songs or nursery rhymes that the children would recognise. Write them on slips of paper/cards.

The aim of the game is to recognise a song when played on the kazoo.

You could play this as one big group. Invite a volunteer to the front. Give them a card and a kazoo. They then need to 'kazoo that tune'. Whoever guesses correctly takes the next turn.

Alternatively, with older children you could run this as a quiz in groups. One leader plays each tune in turn, while the teams write down their answer.

LITTLE BIG QUESTION

What's your favourite worship song and why?

LITTLE BIG IDEA

ILLUSTRATION: SING TO THE LORD!

The best way to learn about praise is to do it!

Invite a worship leader in to talk to the children about why we sing praises to God, and lead the children in some simple songs as part of it.

Alternatively you could play the **session Bible verse** to open the theme, or have an extended time of singing and dancing to God using the **Little Worship Company Praise Party** programme found on the DVD main menu: *Play: PRAISE PARTY.* DVD

MESSAGE

- Think about the best news you ever heard. How does it make you feel? What does it make you do?
- When you get good news, it's hard to stay quiet. You want to cheer and sing as loudly as you can. Happy news makes us want to clap our hands and jump around!
- The best news of all is that God made us, loves us, and is always with us. That's why for hundreds and thousands of years, people have been singing praises to God.
- The Bible is packed full of people praising God. Whenever they see how brilliant He is, they burst into song.
- They aren't the only ones. The Bible says that angels sing praises to God too, day and night.
- The Bible says, "Sing to the Lord a new song; everybody sing to the Lord!" (Psalm 96:1). Today, in this church, and all over the world, children, women and men who love God are singing songs to tell Him how wonderful He is, and to show how thankful they are for all the good things He gives to them. And we will too.
- God loves to hear us sing praises to Him. So let's sing and cheer and jump and dance to God!

LET'S WORSHIP

Song: *Sing to the Lord*

Singalong: *Joy*

Prayer: Praise Party thank you prayer

LITTLE GROUPS

SING TO THE LORD A NEW SONG

You will need: *pens, paper*

Work in groups to create a new song of praise.

Talk to the children about some of the things they want to say to God. It might be about who He is and what He's like (e.g. big, good), or it might be something they want to say thank you for (e.g. loving us).

Use a simple, familiar tune – for example, *Twinkle, Twinkle, Little Star.* Write some words to fit the tune. (It doesn't need to rhyme!)

Sing them together as part of the session. Why not use them in later weeks too?

SESSION PRAYER

Dear God, thank you for loud voices to sing to You. Thank you for bouncy legs to dance to You. Thank you that You are so amazing, so kind, and so loving. **Amen.**

GET CRAFTY!

Difficulty level
suitable for all ages · for older children

We can praise God by dancing too! Use these crafts to get your children dancing to God.

1 SENSORY PAINT PLAY

You will need: *lots of big paper, paint*

- Lay a roll of paper out on the floor (or stick down big sheets).
- Let the children stand in the paint and then dance over the paper.
- They can make footprints and see the colourful paint marks they can make by moving.

Make sure this activity is well supervised. Don't forget to keep a basin of warm water on hand to wash painty feet!

2 DVD SPIN DRUM

You will need: *paper plates, colouring pens, a stick (or similar), glue, sticky tape, hole punch, string, beads*

Each child will need two paper plates.

To make the spin drum:

- Decorate the underneath of the plate with colouring pens.
- Turn one plate over. Lay a long stick down the middle to make a handle, and tape it into place.
- Glue around the edges of the plate and stick the other plate straight on top with the colourful side up.
- Use a hole punch to make two holes on each side of the plate, then thread a piece of string through each hole. Each length of string should be about 25cm long.
- Thread some beads through and tie the string tightly.
- Once the glue is set, spin the stick in your hands to make a drum sound. Use it to make rhythms to dance to God!

3 WINDMILLS

You will need: *paper (in large squares), decorating materials, split pins, straws, plasticine, sharp pencil, scissors*

Each child will need a square of paper.

To make the windmill:

- Decorate both sides of the paper.
- Fold the paper on both the diagonals.
- Cut down each of the diagonal lines from the corners to about 3cm off the centre point.
- There will be two flaps at each corner. Bend one of each carefully into the middle.
- Once all four triangles are in place, lay the windmill onto a blob of plasticine. Then, with a very sharp pencil, pierce through all the layers to make a hole.
- Thread a split pin through the hole. Open it up and grip it around the top of a straw.
- Work your windmill around a few times to make sure it moves smoothly.

Invite the children to put their windmills in the garden. Whenever they see them move and dance in the wind, it will remind them to move and dance to God too!

PP2
Sing to the LORD a new song!
Psalm 96:1
LWC
Little WORSHIP Company
littleworshipcompany.com

3 Praise God with loud instruments

In this session, the children will:

- explore praising God by making music to Him

Based on Psalm 150:3-5 (LWC)

Praise God – He is so great! Praise Him with the loud trumpet. Praise Him with guitars and violins. Praise Him with drums and whistles. Praise Him with tamboures and maracas!

ICE-BREAKER

Preparation level

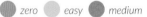

 *zero*  *easy* *medium*

GAME: THE RHYTHM GAME

In this game, the leader claps a simple rhythm. Can the children clap it back?

To make it more complicated, you could turn it into a memory game by adding new rhythms onto the end of the existing rhythm. How long can you make your rhythm?

Alternatively, you could play a quick round of 'Air Band Musical Statues'.

Play some music. Instead of dancing, the children must pretend to play along to the music on imaginary instruments. When the music stops, they must freeze in a musical pose (i.e. as if playing their instrument). Praise the best poses!

LITTLE BIG QUESTION

What's your favourite instrument and why?

LITTLE BIG IDEA

ILLUSTRATION: PRAISE HIM WITH WONDERFUL INSTRUMENTS! 

There's a lot of scope in this session for the children to learn about praise by doing it!

To set the scene, you might like to invite a musician from the church to share why they love praising God using their instrument.

Ask them about their instrument. It would be good if they could demonstrate how it works and, if appropriate, let the children try it themselves.

You might like to collect as many different instruments as possible ahead of your worship time – including any made by the children as part of their craft.

You or a musician in the church could lead the children in making new music and rhythms, or have an extended time of singing and dancing to God using the **Little Worship Company** **Praise Party** programme found on the DVD main menu: *Play: PRAISE PARTY*. The **session Bible verse,** found on the DVD, can also be introduced here.

MESSAGE

- Reflect on some of the different instruments the children know about. What are their favourites? Do any of the children play an instrument?
- There are so many different instruments we can choose from. Some you hit – like big, loud drums. Some you shake – like jingling bells and tambourines. Some you blow – like trumpets, recorders and kazoos. Some you strum – like guitars. We can use all of these instruments to praise God.
- People have been making music to God for thousands of years. [Read out Psalm 150, reflecting on all the different instruments found in the list.]
- Churches are full of instruments that can make big, beautiful sounds to God – from grand organs and pianos, to electric guitars and drums.
- Sometimes music can show our feelings better than words can. We might not know how to tell God we love Him. But we can make a happy noise to show Him!

LET'S WORSHIP

Song: *Shake-a-hallelujah*
Singalong: *Joy*
Prayer: **Praise Party** thank you prayer

LITTLE GROUPS

JAM JAR PRAISE!

You will need: *some jam jars or glass bottles, water, stick beaters (pencils will do!)*

Give each child their own jam jar. Fill each jar with different amounts of water to create different pitches.

As a group, play your jam jar instruments to praise God.

- Invite each child to beat their instrument in turn, up and down the row.
- 'Conduct' the children to play in different orders – for example, when you point at them, they play! Try playing two or three at a time to see what sounds you can make.
- Can you make up a tune as a group?

After they've had some practice, invite the entire jam jar orchestra to play along to some worship music.

SESSION PRAYER:

Dear God, thank you for beautiful music. Thank you for all the different sounds we can make for You. Help us to praise You wherever we are and whatever we're doing. **Amen.**

GET CRAFTY!

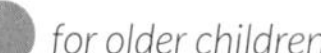

Difficulty level

It's good to praise God with instruments. Invite the children to make some of their own with these crafts!

1 TRUMPET

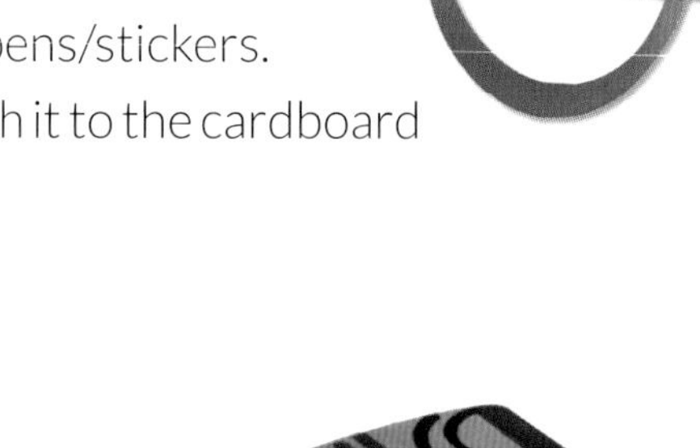

You will need: *cardboard rolls, card, decorating materials, sticky tape*

To make the trumpet:

- Decorate your cardboard roll with paint/pens/stickers.
- Make a cone out of a strip of card and attach it to the cardboard roll with tape.
- Add a strip of card to make a handle.

2 CASTANETS

You will need: *thick card, decorating materials, some copper coins (1p or 2p) or bottle tops, sticky tack*

To make the castanets:

- Fold a 10cm long strip of thick card in half.
- Decorate one side with pens and stickers.
- On the other side, attach two coins or two bottle tops to each end using sticky tack.
- Play the castanets by clicking them together using your fingers.

3 SHAKERS

You will need: *paper plates, decorating materials, dried beans, glue or stapler, ribbons, hole punch (optional)*

To make the shaker:

- Decorate the underneath of the plate.
- Fold it in half and put some dried beans in the middle.
- Staple or glue around the sides.
- To make the shaker really colourful, punch some holes around the side and thread some colourful ribbons through it.

Praise God...
He is so great!
Little WORSHIP Company
PP3
LWC Psalm 150:3

4 Praise God with great big THANK YOUS!

In this session, the children will:

- explore praising God by saying thank you to Him

Psalm 136:1 (LWC)

Say a great big THANK YOU to God! He is so good to us! His love never, EVER runs out!

ICE-BREAKER

Preparation level

GAME: WOULD YOU RATHER...?

Use this game of *Would you rather...?* to introduce some of the wonderful things we have to be thankful for in this world: creation, food and drink, friends and family, etc.

To play the game, pose a 'Would you rather...?' question. Ask the children to show their opinion by moving to different areas of the room. Ask a few to explain their thinking each time.

Suggested questions: Would you rather...

- climb a mountain or swim in the ocean?
- only ever eat dinner or only ever eat pudding?
- play on a sunny beach or play in the snow?
- have a party with your friends or a trip to a theme park with your family?
- have a pet lizard or a pet parrot?

LITTLE BIG QUESTION

Who was the last person you said thank you to, and why?

LITTLE BIG IDEA

ILLUSTRATION: THANK YOU BAG

You will need: *a large bag or suitcase, and some items that represent different things you might be thankful for – for example, food items, pictures of family and friends, a plant to represent nature*

Explain to the children that we are thinking about praising God by saying 'thank you'. Ask them: are there any things they are thankful for?

Show them your bag. Explain that you have been collecting things that you are thankful for. Bring out the items one at a time, discussing them with the children.

For example, bring out your food item:

- What is it? Who likes this too?
- What are your favourite kinds of food? Why?
- Why is food so important to us?

MESSAGE

- We have been thinking about praising God. Praising God is our way of telling God how brilliant He is and how much we love Him.
- The Bible tells us to "Say a great big THANK YOU to God" (Psalm 136:1). One way of praising God is thanking Him for all the amazing things He has done for us and for all the great things He gives to us.
- We can thank God for the wonderful world we live in. The Bible says that God made it. Sun, moon, stars, animals, birds, fish, forests and rivers – they're all here because God put them here.
- We can thank God for looking after us. The Bible says that God gives us the food we need to eat and the clothes we need to wear. He also gives us His peace when we feel worried and helps us when we need to be brave.
- We can thank God for His BIG love for us. The Bible says that we know God loves us because – best of all – He gave us Jesus. Because of Jesus, we can be friends with God forever, knowing He is always by our side. And that's worth the biggest THANK YOU of them all!

LET'S WORSHIP

Song: *Happy Day*
Singalong: *Joy*
Prayer: Praise Party thank you prayer

LITTLE GROUPS

PRAYER BALL

You will need: a lightweight or sponge ball

Sit in a circle. Ask the children to think quietly about some of the things that they're thankful for.

- It might be a person, a thing, or a hobby they have.
- It might be something or someone that makes them really happy or keeps them healthy.
- It might be an experience that they have had.

Share the ideas by rolling the ball across the circle. Whoever catches it shares one thing that they want to say thank you for. They then pass it onto somebody else who shares in turn.

At the end, say a great big THANK YOU to God for all the things He gives us.

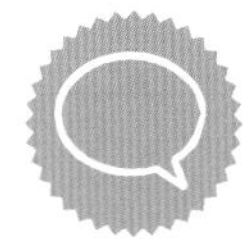

SESSION PRAYER

Dear God, thank you for all the wonderful things You give to us. Thank you for food and clothes, for friends and family. Thank you that You sent Jesus so that we can always be Your friends. **Amen.**

GET CRAFTY!

Difficulty level

suitable for all ages · for older children

We praise God every time we thank Him. Use these activities to help your children to praise God with 'thank yous' now and every day.

1 THANKFULNESS COLLAGE

You will need: *a long roll of paper, pens or pencils*

Lay a long sheet of paper out. Invite the children to write or draw different things they want to thank God for on the roll.

2 THANKFULNESS JAR

You will need: *jars (e.g. empty jam jars), craft (lollipop) sticks, decorating materials, glue*

To make your thankfulness jar:

- Decorate the jar with ribbons, feathers, beads, sequins, etc.
- Use craft sticks to write or draw things you are thankful for.
- Put them in your decorated jar.

Pull out different sticks throughout the week and thank God for whatever's written on them.

3 DVD THANKFULNESS PEACOCK

You will need: *green A4 paper, cardboard tubes, paint, glue, googly eyes, spare paper*

Each child will need one sheet of green A4 paper and a cardboard tube.

To make a thankfulness peacock:

- Finger-paint the green sheet of paper with blue and yellow paint to make peacock feathers.
- Write things you are thankful for on the feathers.
- When it's dry, concertina it up along the long side, then fold it in half and glue together.
- Make the peacock's body by painting a cardboard tube blue. Add a yellow beak and some googly eyes.
- Attach it to the feathers with some glue.

God's love
never
ever
runs
out!
Draw some
of the people
you love!
Psalm 136:1
LWC
Little
WORSHIP
Company
PP4

5 Praise God with following footsteps

In this session, the children will:

- explore the idea of a 'life of worship' – praising God by what we do as well as what we say
- understand that we can praise God by following Jesus' commands and example

Ephesians 5:1 (LWC)

See what God does, and then go and do it yourself!

ICE-BREAKER

Preparation level

zero easy medium

GAME: JUST DANCE!

Lead your own 'aerobic' warm-up with the children. They must copy everything you do in time to music.

If you have an appropriate console or internet access, you might choose to use a game such as *Just Dance Kids* rather than lead it yourself.

Tip: For a low-tech alternative, play a few rounds of *Simon Says* with the children.

LITTLE BIG QUESTION

Who is your hero? If you could be like anybody, who would it be and why?

LITTLE BIG IDEA

ILLUSTRATION: THE TIME MACHINE

You will need: a few first-century costumes and props, bread, music, chocolate coins

Note: you will need one or more people to help you lead this.

Run a short sketch in which you and the children go back in time to the first century and bump into different people who encountered Jesus.

A suggested script outline can be found in the appendix.

LINK TO MESSAGE

To introduce the message, you might like to play *Follow Him* from the DVD. 

MESSAGE

- We've been thinking about the different ways we can praise God and show Him we love Him.
- We can tell God that we love Him by the things we say. We can sing songs of praise to sing thank you to Him for all the good things He gives to us. But we can also show God that we love Him with the things we do.
- The Bible says, "See what God does, and then go and do it yourself!" (Ephesians 5:1). In other words, one of the best ways of showing our love for God is by doing the things He does.
- To help us do this, we need to look at Jesus, His Son. Jesus shows us what God is like. Jesus fed people when they were hungry. He made sick people better. He was a good friend to people who were sad and lonely – and He even made friends with people that nobody else liked.
- We can praise God and show Him how much we love Him by watching Jesus and following in His footsteps. And we don't actually need a time machine to do this! There are lots of stories about Jesus in the Bible. The more we read about Jesus, the more we will understand how God wants us to live.

LET'S WORSHIP

Song: *Joyful Joyful*
Singalong: *He's Got the Whole World in His Hands*
Prayer: Praise Party thank you prayer

LITTLE GROUPS

STORIES OF JESUS

In groups, talk to the children about the stories of Jesus that they are familiar with.

- Which ones do they know?
- What do these stories tell them about what Jesus is like?
- What would it mean for us to 'do likewise'?

Tip: If the children are too young to know or remember any, then you may like to read one or two stories of Jesus from a children's Bible together. Reflect on the questions above after reading.

SESSION PRAYER

Dear God, thank you for Jesus. Thank you for all the amazing things that He said and did. Help us to be more like Jesus and to follow in His footsteps. Amen.

GET CRAFTY!

Difficulty level
suitable for all ages *for older children*

Jesus shows us what it means to live a life of worship. Use these crafts to remind the children to look to Jesus and follow where He leads.

1 BINOCULARS

You will need: *cardboard tubes, paints, glue, strips of paper, decorating materials, ribbon*

Each child will need two cardboard tubes (e.g. kitchen rolls).

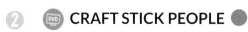

To make your binoculars:

- Paint the tubes a bright colour.
- Glue a 10cm by 30cm piece of paper and wrap it around the two tubes to fix them together.
- Decorate them with stickers, jewels, etc. Attach a length of ribbon as a strap.

As you make the craft, think about the different things we see Jesus doing in the gospels.

2 DVD CRAFT STICK PEOPLE

You will need: *sticks (i.e. gathered from the park), glue, pieces of fabric, wool, googly eyes*

The first followers of Jesus were the disciples. Invite the children to make some stick disciples as a reminder to listen to Jesus' words and to do what they see Him do.

To make your stick person:

- Make some clothes by wrapping fabric around the stick and gluing it into place.
- Make some hair with wool. Glue the top of the stick and tie woolly hair all over the stick person.
- Stick two googly eyes onto its head and make a smile out of red wool.

3 FOOTPRINTS

You will need: *card, pens, scissors, decorating materials, pre-printed Bible verses of Ephesians 5:1 ("See what God does – and then go and do it yourself.")*

To make your footprints:

- Draw around your feet onto card.
- Cut each footprint out.
- Stick the Bible verse onto one footprint, or half onto each.
- Decorate the footprints as you wish.

As you make the footprints, talk about what it means to follow in Jesus' footsteps.

PP5
See what
God does...
then go and
do it
yourself!
Little WORSHIP Company
Ephesians 5:1 LWC

6 Praise God with helpful hands

In this session, the children will:

- explore the story of the Good Samaritan
- understand that we praise God by showing His love to other people

Romans 12:10-13 (LWC)

Always love one another. Be joyful and faithful and patient. Share with people in need. Practise being kind.

ICE-BREAKER

Preparation level

zero easy medium

GAME: PASS THE BALLOON

Play a round of *Pass the Balloon* with the children.

Break the children into groups and ask them to stand in a line.

At the beginning of the game, the person at the front of the line (the captain) holds the balloon. They must pass the balloon to the person behind them by passing it overhead. The next person passes the balloon to the person behind them through their legs. That person then passes it behind them overhead, and so on.

When the balloon reaches the final person in the team, that person runs to the front and the process begins again. The game finishes when the captain makes it back to the front of the line.

In the end, declare the team that you thought was kindest to each other as the winner – rather than the team that was quickest to complete the challenge. (You can draw on this later as part of the Little BIG Idea.)

LITTLE BIG QUESTION

What's the kindest thing you've ever done for somebody else? (Or that somebody did for you?)

LITTLE BIG IDEA

ILLUSTRATION: THE 'GOOD NEWS/BAD NEWS' GOOD SAMARITAN

***You will need:** the **'Good News/Bad News' Good Samaritan** sheet, found in the appendix*

Explore Jesus' parable of the Good Samaritan, found in Luke 10:30-35.

To make the story interactive, read the **Little Worship Company** version found in the appendix.

MESSAGE

- Have you ever had something so good that you really wanted to share it with other people?
- The Bible says that God really loves us. But He doesn't just love us. His love is big enough for EVERYBODY in the whole world. And He wants them to know it!
- We have been looking at different ways of praising God. We can tell God we love Him with songs and prayers and we can show Him we love Him by learning to follow Jesus and by sharing His love with those around us.
- The story of the Good Samaritan is found in the Bible. It's a story that Jesus told to remind us that we show God that we love Him by helping other people.
- Every time we help people in need, we make God happy. Every time we do kind things for others, we make God happy.
- What's more, our kind and helpful actions will make other people happy – and show them how much God loves them too!
- You might like to show the **session Bible verse,** found on the DVD, here. 

LET'S WORSHIP

Song: *Because of Your Love*
Singalong: *He's Got the Whole World in His Hands*
Prayer: Praise Party thank you prayer

LITTLE GROUPS

STEPS OF KINDNESS

You will need: postcards, pens

Invite the children to write a card full of kind words to encourage somebody that they know. It could be someone in their family, a teacher, or a friend.

SESSION PRAYER

Dear God, thank you that Your love for us is really BIG! Help us to share Your love with other people so that they can see how much You love them too. **Amen.**

GET CRAFTY!

Difficulty level

suitable for all ages · for older children

We show our love for God every time we share it with others. Make these crafts and use them to bless other people.

1 HANDPRINT FLOWERS

You will need: *big paper, paint, pens*

To make your handprint flowers:

- Paint your hands in colourful paints.
- Print them on the top of a big sheet of paper.
- Wash hands. Join the handprints together with green lines to make a bunch of flowers.
- Finish it off by painting a vase and some leaves.

Invite the children to give the flowers away to someone they want to thank or encourage.

2 KINDNESS CARDS

You will need: *A4 card, pens, decorating materials*

To make the card:

- Fold a piece of card in half.
- Draw a picture or decorate it with stickers, glitter, etc.

Invite the children to write a kind and encouraging message in the card and to give it to somebody they know.

3 KINDNESS BISCUITS

You will need: *plain biscuits (e.g. rich tea or digestives), icing sugar, water, sprinkles and/or icing pens; paper plates, napkins to take away*

Preparation: Make icing for the biscuits by mixing a few drops of water with icing sugar.

To make your kindness biscuits:

- Cover the biscuits with icing.
- Decorate them using sprinkles (or, with older children, icing pens).
- Put the biscuits on a paper plate with a napkin.

Encourage the children to give the biscuits to a neighbour as an act of kindness.

littleworshipcompany.com

7 Praise God with all of my friends

In this session, the children will:

- explore what happens at church on a Sunday
- understand church as a place to praise God with others

(LWC, inspired by Ecclesiastes 3)

There is a time for everything. A time to play, a time to sleep, a time to read, a time to bounce, a time to eat and a time to party!

ICE-BREAKER

Preparation level

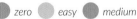

GAME: PRAISE PARTY PICTIONARY

You will need: *a whiteboard or flipchart/large paper, appropriate pens, prepared cards*

Preparation: Create some cards in advance that feature elements of a praise party. Suggestions include balloons, people, guitars [and/or other instruments your children are familiar with], flags, the Bible, etc.

To play, one person is given a card. They must draw the object named on the card on the whiteboard or paper, while the rest of the group guesses what it is. The person who guesses correctly draws the next object.

Tip: With larger groups, you might like to play the game in teams. Create several sets of cards. One player from each team comes to the session leader to collect their first drawing challenge. When it's been guessed correctly, another team member comes to the session leader to collect the next challenge, and the process begins again. Keep playing until one team completes all the challenges.

LITTLE BIG QUESTION

What's the best party you've ever been to and why?

LITTLE BIG IDEA

ILLUSTRATION: ON THE BUS!

You will need: *a slide show of different places – make these age appropriate*

With younger children, you might choose places like the park, a playgroup, the zoo, or a hospital. With older children, you might choose places like a school, a theme park, a birthday party, etc.

Whatever the age, include a picture of your church as your final slide.

Explain that you are going on an adventure. Get into your (imaginary) bus together. Start the engine. (With younger children you might like to ding the bell, etc.) Stop the bus at different locations depicted on your slide show.

Ask the children questions about your different stops.

- Where is this place?
- Who's been to this place, or would like to go there?
- What happens here? Why do people go to this place?

The final stop will be your church. What do the children understand about why they come to church each week?

LINK TO MESSAGE

We go to different places for different reasons. Church is a place to meet with God and to give Him praise.

You might like to show the **session Bible verse,** found on the DVD, here. 

MESSAGE

- The world is full of places that people go to for special reasons.
- There is a special reason we come to church too. We come along to church to praise God and tell Him we love Him. We make time each week to meet with other people who love God too, to celebrate how good He is.
- When we come to church, we praise God by singing, clapping, and dancing to Him. We say 'thank you' to God in our prayers. We also learn about Jesus, so that we know how to live a life that makes God happy during the week.
- This isn't to say that we can't praise God at home. We can! And it doesn't mean we can only praise God on a Sunday. We can praise God any day of the week! But there are some things so amazing that they deserve a special celebration.
- A birthday party is a special way of saying that someone is really brilliant. In the same way, coming to church is a way of giving God special honour. We put down playing, and eating, and sleeping, and all the other things we might do, to come together and celebrate God in a big praise party – because He's worth it!

LET'S WORSHIP

Song: *Celebrate*

Singalong: *He's Got the Whole World in His Hands*

Prayer: Praise Party thank you prayer

LITTLE GROUPS

PRAISE PARTY INVITATIONS

You will need: *the 'Praise Party invitation' worksheet (found in the appendix), pens*

Everybody is invited to God's praise party!

Give the children an invitation each. Let them fill in the blanks with their own praises to God.

SESSION PRAYER:

Dear God, thank you for praise parties! Thank you for special times to jump and sing to You with friends. Thank you, too, that every day with You is special, because You are our friend. **Amen.**

GET CRAFTY!

Difficulty level

suitable for all ages *for older children*

Use these crafts to help the children to remember how good it is to praise God together at church – and to prepare for next session's praise party!

1 ENVELOPE CHURCH

You will need: *brown envelopes, paper, pens, glue, craft (lollipop) sticks*

Each child will need an envelope and a sheet of paper.

To make your envelope church:

- Stick the envelope on the paper with the fold opened up.
- Draw a cross on the top and some doors on the side to make the envelope into a church.
- To make people, draw faces on the sticks and give them some clothes using pens.
- Put them inside the envelope so they can praise God with each other.

2 THANKFULNESS PAPER CHAIN

You will need: *strips of colourful card, sticky tape or glue*

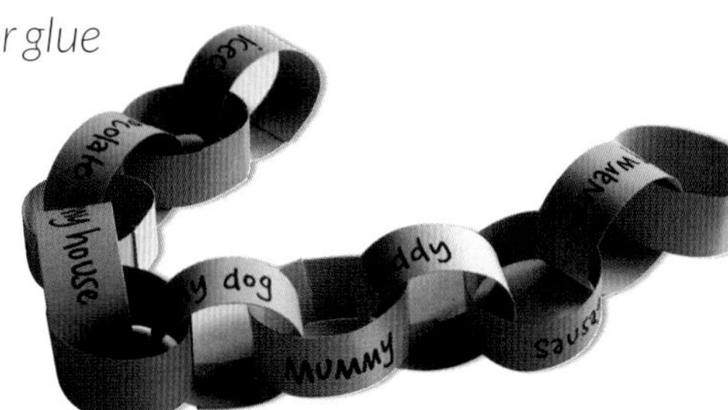

To make your thankfulness chain:

- Take a handful of strips of card.
- Write (or draw) what or who you are thankful for on each strip.
- Make the first link in the chain by sticking two ends of a strip together.
- Make other links by looping each strip into the chain and taping the two ends together.

You might like to link all the chains together to make one big praise paper chain. Keep them for the **Session 8 praise party.**

3 PAPER-CHAIN PEOPLE

You will need: *a long sheet of brown paper (cut into strips about 15cm wide), pens, stickers*

To make the paper-chain people:

- Fold a strip of paper backwards and forwards in a concertina.
- On the top, draw the shape of a person, making sure that the hands of each person reach right to the edge of the fold.
- Cut around the person shape.
- Open the zigzag friends. Decorate them with colourful stickers and pens.

Either: let the children take them home as a reminder of being at church, praising God with their friends; or keep them as decorations for the Session 8 praise party.

There is a time for everything.
Ecclesiastes 3 LWC
Little WORSHIP Company
PP7

8 Praise God with everything I've got!

In this session, the children will:

- enjoy a big praise party!

Psalm 146:2 (LWC)

I'm gonna praise God my whole life long! I'll sing to God for as long as I'm alive!

INTRODUCTION TO THE SESSION

Throughout the **Praise Party** series, the children have explored the subject of praise: why we praise God and how we can praise God.

This final session of the series allows children to experience a praise party for themselves! They will have the opportunity to praise God in a number of different ways explored over previous weeks – from singing and dancing, to saying thank you, to finding ways of helping others.

You will need to ensure that there are adequate numbers of adults in attendance to support the children in each area.

Tip: If you are running this with younger children, you might like to do a 'mini' version of this within a wider free play context. In this scenario:

- Create a party environment within your space – e.g. with lights and balloons.
- Have instruments/dance props ready for use.
- Play **Praise Party Mix** (the Looyahs' praise party) DVD – or, if you are short of time, you could just play the Looyahs' introduction to the praise party and this session's song, *Dance Dance* – inviting the children to join in with music and dance; and/or play the **Praise Party** **Singalongs.**
- Use this week's **Session Prayer** or the **Praise Party** thank you prayer (found on the DVD).
- Set out a range of crafts that touch on the different 'praise' themes, either from the **Praise Party** suggestions or the **Get Crafty!** section.

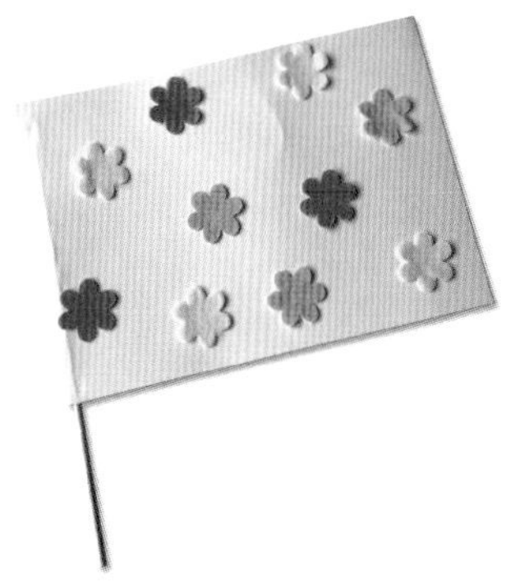

RUNNING THE PRAISE PARTY

Prepare different areas around the room reflecting the following themes:

- music and movement
- adoration and thankfulness
- acts of kindness

Depending on the size of your group, you may like to:

- invite the children to visit any or all of the different areas over the course of the praise party, as many times as they would like to; OR
- break the group into three and allocate them 10-15 minutes at each area

1 MUSIC AND MOVEMENT

This is an area where children can sing, dance and make music to God.

You might like to set the scene by having twinkly lights, disco lights or even a bubble machine running. You may also like to put a few balloons up!

Get out a box of instruments, such as shakers and tambourines, and/or dance ribbons for the children to use along to the music.

Play the **Little Worship Company** Praise Party programme (found on the DVD main menu: *Play: PRAISE PARTY)* DVD in full, either on TV or projected onto a large screen. Invite the children to sing and dance along.

Tip: Why not add to the party atmosphere by offering face-painting?

2 ADORATION AND THANKFULNESS

This is an area where children can express their love and thankfulness for all God has done.

Put out a large roll of paper and pens. Invite the children to write prayers or draw things to God.

Put out copies of the **Session 8** colouring sheet.

Create some thank you balloons for the praise party by inflating balloons and writing or drawing things you are thankful for on the balloons.

In addition, you might like to use some of the 'thankfulness' crafts outlined in **Session 4: Praise God with great big THANK YOUS!**

3 ACTS OF KINDNESS

This is an area where the children can engage in different activities that can be used to share God's love with others.

Use some of your favourite ideas from **Session 6: Praise God with helpful hands.**

Create a generosity jar by decorating jars or yoghurt pots. Use them to collect any stray pennies or change that can go to a good cause.

Put out copies of the **kindness wallchart** found in the appendix. Encourage the children to think of a different act of kindness they could do every day for the next week to share God's love with those around them, and then to write it into their chart.

GET CRAFTY!

Difficulty level

suitable for all ages · for older children

In addition to the above, you might like to use these praise-themed crafts as part of the session.

1 PRAISE FLAG

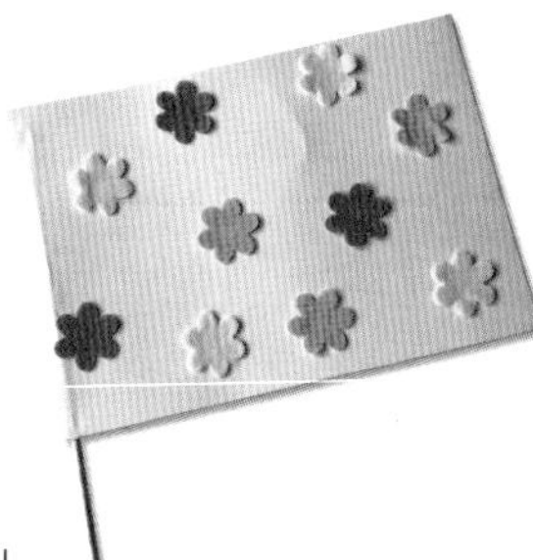

You will need: *an A4 sheet of paper, decorating materials, a straw or dowel*

To make the flag:

- Decorate a piece of A4 paper.
- Attach it to a straw or dowel. Then wave it to praise God!

2 PRAISE BUNTING

You will need: *triangular-shaped paper, string, pegs or staples*

To make the bunting:

- Take one or two triangles.
- Draw or write things you are thankful for or want to praise God for.
- Attach them to a long piece of string with pegs or staples to make praise bunting which can be hung up for the praise party.

3 SHAVING FOAM PRAISE BAG

You will need: *a ziplock bag, marker pens, shaving foam, food colouring in different shades*

Each child will need their own ziplock bag.

To make the foam praise bag:

- Decorate the ziplock bag with the marker pens.
- Squirt shaving foam into the bag.
- Add some drops of food colouring to the bag and zip it closed tightly.
- Enjoy squishing the sensory bag until the foam is all coloured.

SESSION PRAYER

Dear God, thank you that You are **greater** than we can imagine. Thank you that Your love for us is **bigger** than we can imagine. Help us to keep on praising You our whole lives long! **Amen.**

Psalm 146:2
LWC
I'm gonna
praise God
my whole life long!
Little
WORSHIP
Company
PP8

PRAISE PARTY
All-age worship

At the end of the curriculum course, you may like to lead a Sunday morning, all-age worship service on the curriculum's theme, inviting the children to participate in leading it.

Follow or adapt the service plan below as appropriate for your congregation.

WELCOME

Welcome the congregation to the service.

OPENING PRAYER

Dear God, we've come here [this morning] to praise You. We're going to sing to You. We're going to dance to You. We're going to say great big **thank yous** to You.

We want to make You smile this morning as we show You how brilliant You are and how much we love You. **Amen.**

WORSHIP

Sing a couple of **songs** from the **Praise Party** DVD. 

Say this **child-friendly prayer** together. Invite the children – big ones as well as little ones! – to join in with some actions as you read.

ALL-AGE LITURGY

Thank you, God, for praise parties!

Thank you for my great friends.

Thank you that I can dance.

Thank you that I can jump up high.

Thank you for my crazy arms.

Thank you for music that makes me spin.

Thank you for swinging hips.

Thank you that I can praise You.

Thank you for my clapping hands.

Thank you, God, for my little worship time!

Amen.

CHILDREN'S SLOT

Invite the children to the front to talk about the different things they have learnt over the last few weeks. They might like to share some of the crafts they have made, or any memory verses they have learnt.

The children may also like to sing a **Praise Party singalong song.** 
Perhaps they could teach it to the adults!

WORD

Read one or more of the suggested **Bible readings** (or choose your own). Invite a range of readers – young and old – to do this.

- **Psalm 150** A call for everything that has breath to praise God.
- **Psalm 146** A personal response to the faithful God who made us and loves us.
- **Colossians 3:12-17** A call to honour God with our attitudes, words and deeds.

MESSAGE

Share the suggested message below or create your own.

Key Bible passage: Psalm 150 (The Message translation)

Key message: We are invited to God's praise party, so that the whole world will come to know and praise Him too.

Preparation: Have a large party invitation set up in a huge envelope. Write the following details on it:

1. **You are invited to a praise party!**
   Praise God for His acts of power, praise Him for His greatness.
2. **Where:** In God's holy house and under open skies.
3. **Who:** Every living, breathing creature.

You might want to cover over some of the details, revealing them as you explain each point. (See corresponding numbers above and below.)

INTRODUCTION

- Ask the congregation about the last and/or best party they went to. What was its purpose? What different kinds of things do we celebrate at parties? Etc.
- Explain that the church has received an invitation to a party too – but what kind of party is it? Who is it for?
- *[Invite some children to help you open the envelope and take a look at what it says.]*

REFLECTION

1. Over the last few weeks the children have been exploring the idea of a Praise Party. **Psalm 150 is an invitation to come and celebrate God.** There are lots of things worth celebrating: birthdays, weddings, anniversaries, and special achievements. But the Bible reminds us that there's something better than all of these things – and that's God. At a praise party, we celebrate all the amazing things He's done for us. *[List a few examples of these.]* We can praise God with singing, dancing, music and stories.
2. This is what the party's for. **But where is it?** We can praise God here – in church, God's holy house. Sundays are special days to meet and celebrate God together – often with instruments and singing. But the Bible says we can praise God anywhere – "under the open skies" (verse 1). We can praise God as we walk around the amazing world He created. We can praise God every time we find something to say 'thank you' for. The more we see Him, the more we want to praise Him – anywhere, anytime.

3 **And who is invited to the praise party?** Everybody! (verse 6) That's because God's love is for everyone. God wants everybody to know Him and the love He has for them – and to come and celebrate Him too. And the louder we praise God and celebrate all He has done, the easier it will be for the world to hear how great God is!

PRAYERS

WALL OF PRAISE

Use this activity as a way of praising God for all the good things He has done/does for us.

You will need: *coloured paper or sticky notes, pens*

- Reflect on the psalms of thanksgiving. They often state truths about God – for example, that He is a provider or refuge; and they list specific things God has done for His people – for example, how He has rescued them or healed them.
- Give out paper and pens. Invite the congregation to think of specific things that they want to praise and thank God for and to write them down.
- After a few minutes, invite them to stick their paper to a 'wall of praise' in the church.
- When they are all assembled, lead the congregation in your own psalm of thanksgiving. Read out a note at a time. After each one, say the following response:
    - **LEADER** "God, You're great..."
    - **CONGREGATION** "...and we love You!"

LIFE OF WORSHIP

We can praise God with our singing and dancing. But we can also praise God with our actions and service. Use this activity as a commitment to love and worship God with every part of us.

You will need: *a large outline of a tree on paper, paint, washing-up bowls of water, towels*

Preparation: Put some paint in a few dishes. Place them at a couple of stations at the front of church. Mount the outline of a tree nearby. (Make sure it's accessible height-wise to the whole congregation.)

- Reflect on how worship is more than what we do at church on a Sunday. It's about choosing to give God our hearts, feet and hands as well as our voices – to love what He loves, to go where He goes, and to do what He does.
- Invite the congregation to respond to the call to live a life of worship by putting their handprint on the tree trunk.
- At the end, reflect on the picture of the now-vibrant tree. Talk about how a life of worship brings life in the world, as people encounter God's love in action.
- Close in prayer.

WORSHIP

Sing one or two songs from the **Praise Party** DVD. (You may like to take up an offering here and/or say the Lord's Prayer together.)

BLESSING AND DISMISSAL

Formally close the service.

CLOSING BLESSING

As we leave this place,
may our voices always be singing,
our feet always following and our hands always helping –
as we praise God with every part of us.
Amen.

THE TIME MACHINE

You will need: *a few first-century costumes/props, bread, music, chocolate coins*

Note: you will need a couple of people (or one person in a range of wigs/costumes) to play Bellyache Ben, Dancing Dave and Thomas. (There is also a brief, optional cameo from Zacchaeus.)

Explain that the Bible says that we can praise God by looking at Jesus and following in His footsteps. So let's go back in time and see what He did!

Mime getting into an imaginary time machine. Jiggle around as you head back through time until you land in the first century.

Meet the following people one at a time:

1 **Bellyache Ben** (a person in a crowd of 5,000 who's just enjoyed Jesus' all-you-can-eat buffet)

2 **Dancing Dave** (a former paralytic healed by Jesus)

3 **Thomas** (one of Jesus' disciples)

[Enter Ben, clutching his tummy.]

LEADER: Hello there! Goodness – are you alright?

BEN: Yes, yes, I'm fine. Just feeling a bit full.

LEADER: Full?

BEN: Alright – about to burst. I think I ate too much.

LEADER: Too much what?

BEN: Bread. And fish. But there was so much there. And it was soooo tasty!

LEADER: What happened? Where were you?

BEN: Have you ever heard of Jesus? Well, he was here on this mountainside. We came to hear him talk and – well – hopefully heal a few people too. He's been doing that a lot lately! There were loads of us – literally thousands and thousands of people. He knows how to draw a crowd! He was so interesting to watch that we forgot how late it was getting. Our tummies didn't, though. You could hear my tummy rumbling a mile off.

LEADER: But I thought you said your tummy hurt because it was full?

BEN: I did. Jesus noticed how hungry we all were. This lad near me gave him his lunch box. It only had five loaves and two fish in it. You wouldn't think that would go very far. But Jesus said a 'thank you' prayer, broke the bread and started giving it out. I had some. And then some seconds. And then, cos it was so delicious, thirds. So did my mates. In fact, that little meal got round FIVE THOUSAND people. And there were still twelve basketfuls left over! Jesus doesn't like to leave anyone hungry – that's for sure. Here – I took a bit for the journey home. Does anyone want some? [Ben hands round the bread and then leaves.]

LEADER: Amazing! Bye bye. I wonder who else we might meet here?

[Enter Dancing Dave. Play some upbeat music and let Dave dance for a minute.]

LEADER: Wow – who are you?

DAVE: My name's Dave. And I looooove to dance!! *[He keeps dancing.]*

LEADER: Have you always loved dancing?

DAVE: Well, believe it or not, only a few months ago, I couldn't dance. I couldn't even walk! I was totally paralysed. But then I met Jesus. He healed me. Just told me to get up and walk. So I did. Just look at me now! *[Dave dances some more.]*

LEADER: That's incredible!

DAVE: Can't stop to chat. Too – busy – dancing!

[Dave leaves, still dancing.]

LEADER: Wow – Jesus has been doing some amazing things! Feeding the hungry... Healing people... Here's somebody else – I wonder if he's met Jesus too?

[Enter Thomas.]

LEADER: Hello! Do you know Jesus?

THOMAS: Yes, I do actually! My name's Thomas. I'm one of Jesus' disciples. I spend pretty much all day, every day with him. He always has interesting things to teach us. Although – just between us – I don't always understand what he's talking about.

LEADER: We keep meeting people with amazing stories about Jesus.

THOMAS: Yes. Life is always a surprise with Jesus! You never know what he might do next. Sometimes, he seems to vanish – and then we find him talking to someone really... weird. You know, the people nobody else will speak to. Like the other day, we found him chatting to a tax collector. Ha! A tax collector! You know – the ones who'll take your last penny and give it to those nasty Romans. There's a reason nobody likes them. But Jesus is always making friends – especially with people everyone else avoids. And they're never the same after they've met Jesus. Oh look – here's that tax collector now... See what I mean? Totally different.

[Enter Zacchaeus, giving out gold coins to the children. Thomas leaves.]

LEADER: Well, that was fun. But time to get back in the time machine...

THE 'GOOD NEWS/BAD NEWS' GOOD SAMARITAN

BASED ON LUKE 10:30-35

Read through the story below. Invite the children to join in at certain words:

- **GOOD – Hooray!** *[Children cheer.]*
- **BAD – Oh, no!** *[Children boo.]*

THE STORY

Once there was a man who was walking from Jerusalem to Jericho. As he wandered through the lonely mountain pass, something **BAD** happened. A group of robbers jumped out on him. They hit him, stole everything he had and left him lying unconscious on the ground. **Oh, no!**

But don't worry. There's **GOOD NEWS.** Just then a priest came along. Everybody knew that priests were **GOOD** and godly men. He'd help the poor man! **Hooray!**

But there's **BAD NEWS.** The priest didn't help him. He just frowned at the man, crossed over to the other side of the road and went on his way. **Oh, no!**

But there's **GOOD NEWS.** Somebody else was coming. A Levite! Levites worked in the temple. They were God's extra special friends. He'd *definitely* help the poor man. **Hooray!**

But there's **BAD NEWS.** The Levite didn't even stop. He just looked a bit sick and hurried past on the other side of the road. **Oh, no.** Whatever would the poor man do?

But there's **GOOD NEWS.** Somebody else was coming. **Hooray!** It's a... it's a...

Uh-oh. **BAD NEWS.** It's a Samaritan. There's no way that he would help. The man on the ground was a Jew and everybody knew that Jews and Samaritans didn't get on. In fact, they hated each other. **Oh, no!**

But what's this? **GOOD NEWS!** The Samaritan stopped. He got down from his donkey, bandaged up the man's wounds and gave him something to drink. **Hooray!**

And there's even more **GOOD NEWS.** He put the man on his donkey and took him to an inn. And he gave the innkeeper enough money to look after the man until he was better. **Hooray!**

REFLECTION

Jesus told this story because somebody had asked Him what pleased God. The priest and the Levite in the story were very good at saying their prayers and singing songs to God. But how good were they at loving the people around them?

Which person do ***you*** *think made God happiest? Why?*

Let's Party!

Decorate an invitation
for your very own Praise Party

To ....

You are invited to

A Praise Party

We are praising God because...

1 ....

2 ....

3 ....

Come to ....

on ....

....

at ....

Kindness Wallchart

	lay the table	make my bed	give a hug	pick up my toys	....	....	....	....
Sunday								
Monday								
Tuesday								
Wednesday								
Thursday								
Friday								
Saturday								

Wonderful Day Bible curriculum

WONDERFUL DAY

The Bible is full of God's good promises to us. **Wonderful Day** helps children to explore what these mean for them today, from the moment they wake up until they go to bed, and what it means for them to love and live for God each day in turn.

1 GOD MADE TODAY

In this session, the children will:

- understand that each day is a special day given by God

This is the day that the Lord has made; let us rejoice and be glad in it. Psalm 118:24 (NRSV)

2 GOD LOVES ME TODAY

In this session, the children will:

- explore different events and emotions we experience each day
- understand that whatever happens, or however we might feel, we can be sure that God loves us and is with us

There's nothing in the world that can separate us from God's great love.
Romans 8:39 (LWC)

3 GOD IS WITH ME TODAY

In this session, the children will:

- understand that God is always with us
- start to explore prayer – what it involves, and why and how we pray

Be close to God and He will be close to you. James 4:8 (LWC)

4 GOD GIVES ME GOOD THINGS TODAY

In this session, the children will:

- reflect on the good things we have and experience each day
- understand them as gifts from God to thank Him for

He has made everything beautiful in its time. Ecclesiastes 3:11

5 GOD GIVES ME ALL I NEED TODAY

In this session, the children will:

- explore the miracle of Jesus' feeding of the 5,000
- reflect on God's promise to provide whatever we need

God is able to give you all you need – and more! 2 Corinthians 9:8 (LWC)

6 GOD GIVES ME A FRESH START TODAY

In this session, the children will:

- reflect on some of the bad choices we might make in the day
- understand that even if we make mistakes, God loves us and gives us another chance

If we say sorry to God when we get something wrong, we can be sure that He will always, always make it right again. 1 John 1:9 (LWC)

7 GOD HOLDS ME IN HIS HANDS TODAY

In this session, the children will:

- explore the story of Jesus calming the storm
- understand that God is bigger than anything that worries us, and that He promises us His peace

Be still and know that I am God. Psalm 46:10

8 GOD IS WITH ME TODAY, TOMORROW AND ALWAYS

In this session, the children will:

- reflect on the promise that God is always with them, even as they sleep

When you go to bed, you will not be scared. When you lie down, your sleep will be sweet. Proverbs 3:24 (LWC)

WORSHIP SONGS

The following worship songs appear in the **Wonderful Day** DVD.

1 *What a Beautiful Name*
2 *10,000 Reasons*
3 *Draw Me Close To You*
4 *Amazing Grace*
5 *Great is Thy Faithfulness*
6 *How Deep the Father's Love*
7 *Hope Song*
8 *Be Still*

SINGALONG SONGS

In addition to these worship songs, there are two fantastic, simple singalong songs for you to learn with your children across the eight weeks.

1 *Walking Down the Street*
2 *Prayer Song*

MEMORY VERSE

Each session has a Bible verse attached, which the children might like to learn each week. These have been written into the photocopiable colouring sheets at the end of each session plan.

Younger children, however, might like to learn just one simple verse across the series. We would suggest this verse from Psalm 118:

This is the day that the Lord has made; let us rejoice and be glad in it.
Psalm 118:24 (NRSV)

① God made today

In this session, the children will:

- understand that each day is a special day given by God

Psalm 118:24 (NRSV)

This is the day that the Lord has made; let us rejoice and be glad in it.

ICE-BREAKER

Preparation level
zero easy medium

GAME: WHAT DAY IS IT?

The aim of the game is for the children to match the special day with its date.

Call out the name of the day (e.g. Christmas Day) and then 4 different options for a date (e.g. December 1st, July 10th, December 25th or 31st May). Get the children to move to different areas of the room, depending on which one they think is the right answer.

Use dates which mean something to the children – for example Mother's Day, the first day of the summer holiday or a birthday of one of the children in the room.

Tip: Depending on the age and stage of your children, you might limit the options to make it easier – e.g. give them 2 choices of date instead of 4.

LITTLE BIG QUESTION

If you could do absolutely anything today, what would it be?

LITTLE BIG IDEA

ILLUSTRATION: JUST AN ORDINARY DAY? 

Explore a typical day with the children.

With younger children, look at different everyday items that they will recognise to talk about their daily experiences.

Preparation: Collect different items that suggest different times in the day – for example, a toothbrush, a rucksack, plates and cutlery, pyjamas, etc. Put them in a suitcase.

Explain that you have packed a few bits and pieces in your case – things that you will need during the day. Look at the items one by one. Try to order the items so that you journey through a day – i.e. look at morning-related items first and conclude with bedtime-related ones. Talk about them with the children.

- What is this? Who has one of these?
- What does this item get used for? When do you use it?

With older children, you might like to create tableaux representing different hours of the day. Break the children into small groups and give each one a time and a day – for example, 8am on a Friday. The group then creates a freeze-frame depicting what they would be doing at that time.

Let each group show theirs in turn, while you commentate on what's happening in each scene.

LINK TO MESSAGE

This may be a typical day. But that doesn't make it ordinary. Every day is special – because it's a day that God has made.

You might like to show the **session Bible verse**, found on the DVD, here. 

MESSAGE

- Ask the children about their idea of the perfect day. What do they love to spend their day doing? (Now would be a good time to share any answers to the little BIG question.)
- Every day is different. But whatever kind of day it is – whether it's a Sunday or a Monday, a 'regular' day or Christmas Day – every day is a special day. That's because it is God's day!
- The Bible says, "This is the day that the Lord has made; let us rejoice and be glad in it." (Psalm 118:24, NRSV). In other words, today – this day – is God's wonderful day. It's a gift He has given to us. And He wants us to enjoy it!
- It also means that God has a special plan for each day too. Today, God wants us to find out a little bit more about Him. Today, God wants us to see Him more and love Him more – wherever we might go and whatever we might do.
- The Bible is full of amazing promises about what it means to spend every day with God by our side. We're going to be looking at these over the next few weeks.
- But for now, let's say a great big thank you to God for this wonderful day He has given us – and let's enjoy it!

LET'S WORSHIP

Song: *What a Beautiful Name*

Singalong: *Walking Down the Street*

Prayer: Wonderful Day thank you prayer

LITTLE GROUPS

TODAY IS GOD'S DAY!

You will need: God's day worksheet *(found in the appendix)*

Over the next few weeks, the children will explore what living each day with God looks like. The purpose of this activity is to encourage the children to recognise God in their everyday situations.

Give each child a copy of the worksheet and explain the challenge – to take some time (possibly at the end of the day) to reflect on where they have seen God and where they have served God each day in the coming week.

Talk together and give practical examples of:

- what it means to see God – e.g. when we feel loved or helped by others; when we are given something brilliant that we like or need; when someone says something encouraging to us
- what it means to serve God – e.g. to do something kind and helpful for other people; to say encouraging things to other people; to give something away

SESSION PRAYER

Dear God, thank you that You made today! Thank you that we can enjoy today. Help us to see You and know You, today and every day. **Amen.**

GET CRAFTY!

Difficulty level

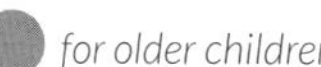

suitable for all ages *for older children*

Use these crafts to help the children remember that today is God's day!

1 SUN PLATE

You will need: *paper plates, small pasta pieces, raw spaghetti, glue*

Each child will need their own paper plate.

To make a sun:

- Decorate a paper plate by sticking yellow pasta in the middle.
- Stick spaghetti 'sunrays' around the edge.

As you make the craft, reflect on how every new sunrise is a new day from God.

2 'DAYS OF THE WEEK' SIGN

You will need: *paper plates, pens and decorating materials, wooden pegs*

Each child will need a paper plate and a peg.

To make the sign:

- Decorate the plate and write the days of the week around the rim. (Note: younger children may need help with this.)
- Draw an arrow on the peg, pointing towards the 'clip' end.
- Peg it onto the plate at the appropriate day.

Encourage the children to thank God for His new day as they move the peg around the plate each morning.

3 DVD STICK HOUSE

You will need: *card, pens or crayons, craft (lollipop) sticks, glue, decorating materials*

Each child will need a sheet of card.

To make the stick house:

- Glue 5 craft sticks onto the card in the shape of a house.
- Write in the words of Psalm 118:24 (LWC) – "God has made this day. Let's be happy and glad about it!"
- Draw in the details of the house using pens or crayons. If there is room, children can draw their family in the house too!
- Put stickers or other decorations onto the house to finish it off.

Encourage the children to display their craft at home and to learn Psalm 118:24 by heart.

This is the day
that the LORD has made!
Psalm 118:24 NRSV
Little
WORSHIP
Company
WD1

2 God loves me today

In this session, the children will:

- explore different events and emotions we experience each day
- understand that whatever happens, or however we might feel, we can be sure that God loves us and is with us

Romans 8:39 (LWC)

There's nothing in the world that can separate us from God's great love.

ICE-BREAKER

GAME: WHAT'S THE TIME, MR WOLF?

You will need a large space to play this game.

In keeping with the theme of 'surprises', play a few rounds of *What's the time, Mr Wolf?*

To play the game, one person acts as the 'wolf'. Mr Wolf stands at one end of the hall with their back turned towards everybody else, whilst the children wait at the other end of the hall.

The children call out, "What's the time, Mr Wolf?" Wolf then replies a time (e.g. 3 o'clock) and the children move forward the appropriate number of steps (in this instance, 3).

The process repeats, until at some point Wolf replies, "Dinner time!" Wolf then turns round and chases the children back to the other end of the hall, trying to catch people on the way.

Tip: If using the game purely as a warm-up, then let the 'caught' person become the next wolf. If playing competitively, then keep the same wolf and ask any 'caught' people to sit out until there is a winner.

LITTLE BIG QUESTION:

What's the biggest surprise you've ever had?

LITTLE BIG IDEA

ILLUSTRATION: WHAT A SURPRISE!

You will need: What a surprise! *scenarios sheet (found in the appendix)*

Each day is full of surprises. Select some everyday scenarios from the list that are appropriate for your children. As you read them out, invite the children to share how that 'surprise' would leave them feeling.

LINK TO MESSAGE

When we wake up in the morning, we don't know what the day will bring. But there's one thing we do know for sure: that we are precious to God.

MESSAGE

- Ask the children to look out of the window. Is today a sunny day or a rainy day? Which kind of day do they prefer?
- Every day is full of surprises – starting with the weather! Sometimes the day ahead is full of exciting surprises. We do all sorts of fun things – and it feels like the best day ever.
- At other times, the day brings a few not-so-good surprises. Sometimes, things might happen that make us feel a bit sad, or a bit worried.
- We might not know exactly what the day will bring. But there's one thing that we can know for sure: that God loves us and is with us every moment of the day.
- We are looking at some of God's good promises to us. One of the most amazing promises is found in Romans 8:39. It says, "There's nothing in the world that can separate us from God's great love." This wonderful promise means that we never need to ask how much God loves us. Every day we can be completely sure that we are really, really special to God!
- It also means that wherever we are each day, and whatever we do, we know that God will be right beside us. God will cheer us on when we're happy. He will hold us if we feel sad. And He will always help us whenever we ask Him.

LET'S WORSHIP

DVD

Song: *10,000 Reasons*

Singalong: *Walking Down the Street*

Prayer: Wonderful Day thank you prayer

LITTLE GROUPS

LOVE HEARTS

You will need: *red craft paper, pens, scissors, decorating materials*

Invite the children to take a piece of craft paper and make a heart by folding it in half, drawing half a heart shape, and cutting it out. Let them write their names in the middle, and/or draw a picture of themselves.

When they have completed the task, ask the children to be still and focus on their love heart. Say the session's verse from Romans a couple of times, slowly. What does this mean for them?

Close with the **session prayer.**

SESSION PRAYER

Dear God, thank you that whether it's a sunny day or a rainy day, You're the same awesome, good and loving God. Thank you that You love us completely and will be beside us today and every day. **Amen.**

GET CRAFTY!

Difficulty level
suitable for all ages · for older children

In sunshine and rain, summer and winter, God always loves us! These crafts will help your children to remember this wonderful promise.

1 UMBRELLA

You will need: *large card, poster paints, water, straws*

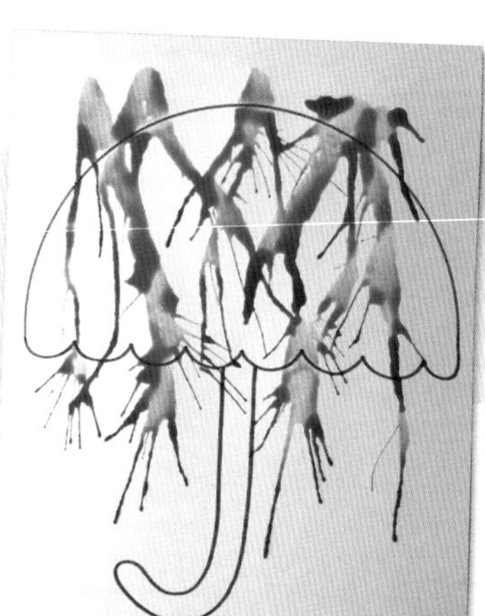

Preparation: Create an umbrella template for older children/adults to use; or cut out ready-to-use umbrella shapes. Add water to poster paints to make them quite watery.

Each child will need a card umbrella.

To decorate:

- Put a few drops of watery paint on the top of the picture.
- Using a straw, blow the paint down the picture to make it look like rain.
- When dry, write the session's Bible verse on the umbrella.

Tip: You might want to make one huge umbrella poster if working with a smaller group.

2 TREE PAINTING

You will need: *card, paints, sticks (twigs or craft sticks), sticky tape*

To make the tree trunk:

- Use tape to attach a stick or twig to the centre of a piece of paper.
- Finger paint 'leaves' around the tree. Use different colours for different seasons: pink and white for spring, green for summer, and red and yellow for autumn.

Tip: Don't forget to have a washing-up bowl of soapy water nearby for easy handwashing!

As you make the craft, think about how God loves us every day, whatever the season.

3 DVD RAINBOW BLOWERS

You will need: *cardboard tubes, string, blue paint, cotton wool, glue, strips of coloured tissue paper, sticky tape*

Each child will need a cardboard tube.

To make the blower:

- Paint the tube with blue paint.
- Once it's dry, glue on fluffy cotton wool to make clouds.
- Attach coloured tissue paper strips to the bottom using sticky tape.
- Add a bit of string to the top in order to hang it up.

As you make the rainbow, talk to the children about promises. What are they? What Bible promises do they know?

WD2
There's nothing in the world
that can separate us from
God's great love.
Romans 8:39 LWC
Little
WORSHIP
Company

3 God is with me today

In this session, the children will:

- understand that God is always with us
- start to explore prayer – what it involves, and why and how we pray

James 4:8 (LWC)

Be close to God and He will be close to you.

ICE-BREAKER

Preparation level: zero, easy, medium

GAME: WACKY RACES

You will need: *a few items to make a simple obstacle course, e.g. cones (or chairs) to mark out a slalom, large hoops big enough to fit two people through*

You will need a large space to play this game.

Preparation: Lay out a simple obstacle course, being careful to minimise any risks.

In keeping with the theme of walking with God each day, this obstacle course is to be completed in pairs.

Break the children into pairs – ideally of a similar height. Run through the requirements of the obstacle course. Explain that the children must keep their arms linked for the duration of the course.

Either run this as several races at the same time (one pair against another) or, if you have limited space, run the race one pair at a time in a time trial.

LITTLE BIG QUESTION

When you have important news, who's the first person you want to tell?

LITTLE BIG IDEA

ILLUSTRATION: PRAYER PHONE

You will need: *a phone*

Bring out your phone and show the children. Ask them:

- What is it?
- What is it used for?

Talk about some of the people who are 'stored' in your phone and why:

- You like to talk to them during the day to tell them your news – funny things, exciting things, important things, etc.
- You might need to get in touch with them during the day because you need their help.

Tip: You might like to set up a slide show of some (not necessarily real) texts that illustrate your points – e.g. a picture of something funny you saw which you wanted to share with someone, a text asking a family member to buy milk on their way home, etc.

LINK TO MESSAGE

Prayer is a way of sharing our day with God. We can talk to Him, a bit like we might talk to our best friend on the phone.

You might like to show the **session Bible verse**, found on the DVD, here. 

MESSAGE

- We are looking at God's special promises to us and what it means to live each day with Him.
- The Bible says, "Be close to God and He will be close to you." (James 4:8). This is an amazing promise that God will always be with us, wherever we are and whatever we are doing.
- The Bible also teaches that we can talk to God. The word that we use for this is 'prayer'. Prayer is talking to God, just like we talk to our friends.
- You don't need to have special words to pray with. You don't even need to say the words out loud – God can hear what's in our hearts.
- God loves it when we share our day with Him. We can tell Him about the things that make us happy or that we are excited about.
- We can tell Him about the things which worry us as well. Wherever we are, and whatever we're doing, He's always there to listen and He cares for us more than we'll ever know.

LET'S WORSHIP

Song: *Draw Me Close To You*

Singalong: *Walking Down the Street*

Prayer: Wonderful Day thank you prayer

LITTLE GROUPS

EVERYDAY PRAYERS

Invite the children to talk about their experience of prayer.

- Have they ever prayed?
- What kinds of things do they pray about?
- Have they ever had any experiences of answered prayer?

If using with older children, you might want to look together at the most famous prayer in the Bible – the Lord's Prayer. What does this prayer teach us about the kinds of things we might say to God/ask God for?

Close with the **session prayer.**

SESSION PRAYER

Dear God, thank you that You promise to always be with us. Thank you that we can talk to You about everything we do and everything we feel, today and every day. **Amen.**

GET CRAFTY!

Difficulty level

suitable for all ages *for older children*

Use these crafts to help the children reflect on what it means for God to be with us each day.

1 FLIP FLOPS

You will need: *paper, strong card, pens, scissors, glue, ribbons, foam shape stickers*

To make your flip flops:

- Draw around your feet or shoes, onto a piece of paper.
- Cut the footprints out and stick them onto a piece of colourful card.
- Cut around the whole picture.
- Add flip flop straps (ribbons) and a colourful shape to finish them off.

You might like to write the session's Bible verse on the flip flops, as a reminder to walk each day with God.

2 PRAYER PHONE

You will need: *strong card, white paper, round stickers or buttons, pens, glue, scissors*

Preparation: If using with younger children, you might want to cut the card and white paper into the appropriate shapes/sizes in advance, or make a template for older children by drawing round your phone.

To make the phone:

- Cut 2 rectangles roughly the size of a phone from the strong card.
- Stick the rectangles together, leaving the plain (i.e. non-branded) side on the outside. This makes the main body of the phone.
- Cut a rectangle from the white paper, a little smaller than the card rectangle.
- Stick the white rectangle into the middle of the card rectangle to make the screen.
- Stick 10 round stickers or buttons onto the paper screen to make the keypad. Number them 1-9 and 0.
- To finish off, decorate the other side of the phone.

If it's helpful, invite the children to use their prayer phone to talk to God each day. What will they talk to Him about?

3 HANDPRINT DOVES

You will need: *card, paints, felt tips*

Note: this activity requires extra adult support and supervision.

To make the dove:

- Paint your hands and print them onto the paper with the thumbs touching.
- At the end of the thumb tips, paint 3 'swooshes' to make the tail.
- At the bottom of the hands, paint or draw a round head and a small beak.

Don't forget to have a washing-up bowl of soapy water nearby for easy handwashing!

As you make the craft, talk about how the Bible shows God's Holy Spirit as a dove. Whenever the children see their dove, they can be reminded that God is with them wherever they go.

Little WORSHIP Company

Be close to God

and He will be close to you.

James 4:8 LWC

WD3

4 God gives me good things today

In this session, the children will:

- reflect on the good things we have and experience each day
- understand them as gifts from God to thank Him for

Ecclesiastes 3:11

He has made everything beautiful in its time.

Preparation level

ICE-BREAKER

GAME: WRAP THE LEADER

You will need: *wrapping paper or newspaper, sticky tape, a bow (optional)*

Break the children into teams. Give each team one adult, some wrapping paper or newspaper, and some sticky tape.

Explain that they will have 3 minutes to wrap up their leader as neatly as possible. At the end of the time, declare your favourite present the winner.

LITTLE BIG QUESTION

What's the best present you've ever been given?

LITTLE BIG IDEA

ILLUSTRATION: PASS THE THANKFULNESS PARCEL

You will need: *a parcel (see below), music*

Preparation: You will need to make a parcel in advance. Make sure the present at the heart of the parcel is something the children can share together, e.g. a bag of sweets. In between the layers, include cards with things which we can be thankful for each day.
Suggestions: food to eat, family, friends, toys, pets, school, sunshine, trees, God

Explain that we are thinking about the good gifts God gives to us each day – and to help us, we are going to play a game of 'pass the parcel'.

To play the game, sit the children in a large circle. Start the music. The children need to pass the parcel around the circle until the music stops. Whoever has the parcel unwraps the top layer. Invite them to read out the card they find in the parcel – or, if playing with younger children, read it out for them.

LINK TO MESSAGE

There are lots of good things we experience every day – all of them gifts from God. You might like to show the session *What has God made beautiful?* from the DVD.

MESSAGE

- Ask the children: What are the best bits of your day? Playing with favourite toys? Going to special places with family or friends? Eating pudding?
- There are all kinds of wonderful things to enjoy every day. And the Bible says that they're all gifts from God.
- The Bible says, "God has made everything beautiful in its time." (Ecclesiastes 3:11) He gives us many, many good things each day, from the food we eat, to our family and friends – even the sunshine, the trees and the flowers around us!
- There is something small but really important we can do whenever somebody gives us something, and that's to say 'thank you'. Saying 'thank you' reminds us of all the good things we have. It also pleases the person who gave something to us!
- So, whatever you do today that makes you feel happy or excited, or whatever great things you eat or enjoy today, remember to say a great BIG thank you to the One who made everything happen – God!

LET'S WORSHIP

Song: *Amazing Grace*

Singalong: *Walking Down the Street*

Prayer: Wonderful Day thank you prayer

LITTLE GROUPS

THANK YOU POEMS

You will need: big paper, pens

As a group, write about the different things you are thankful for each day.
Write them as an acrostic, starting each line with the letters T-H-A-N-K-Y-O-U.

Share them together and use them to praise and thank God.

SESSION PRAYER

Dear God, thank you that You love us so much. Thank you that You give us lots and lots of good things, today and every day! **Amen.**

GET CRAFTY!

Difficulty level
suitable for all ages · for older children

Every day is full of good things from God. Use these crafts to reflect on a few of them!

1 CUPCAKES

Thank God for delicious food as you bake these cupcakes. Why not share them with others too?

Recipe:

- 100g self-raising flour
- 100g caster sugar
- 2 eggs
- 100g melted butter

To make your cupcakes:

- Preheat the oven to 180°C/160°C fan/gas mark 4.
- Mix all the ingredients in a large bowl.
- Spoon into cake cases and bake in the oven for 15 minutes.
- Decorate with icing and sprinkles.

2 TREASURE BOX

You will need: *old shoeboxes, decorating materials, pens*

To make the treasure box:

- Decorate a shoebox with craft materials.
- Label it with your name.
- Use it to keep special things inside.

As you make the craft, reflect on all the different treasures you are thankful for.

3 CREATION JARS

You will need: *empty jam jars, 'nature' materials – feathers, leaves, petals, twigs etc, craft glue*

Each child will need one jar.

To make a creation jar:

- Cover the jar in craft glue.
- Stick on flowers, leaves, etc.
- Put another layer of glue over the top of each item.
- The jar will get more and more wonderful as you decorate it with God's creations.

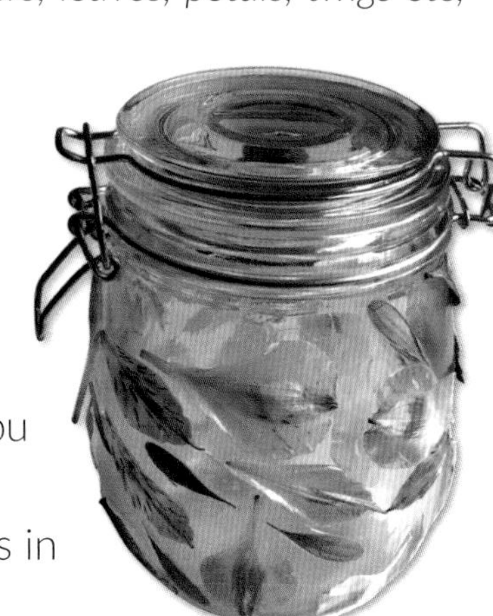

As you make this craft, talk about your favourite things in creation. Thank God for all He has made!

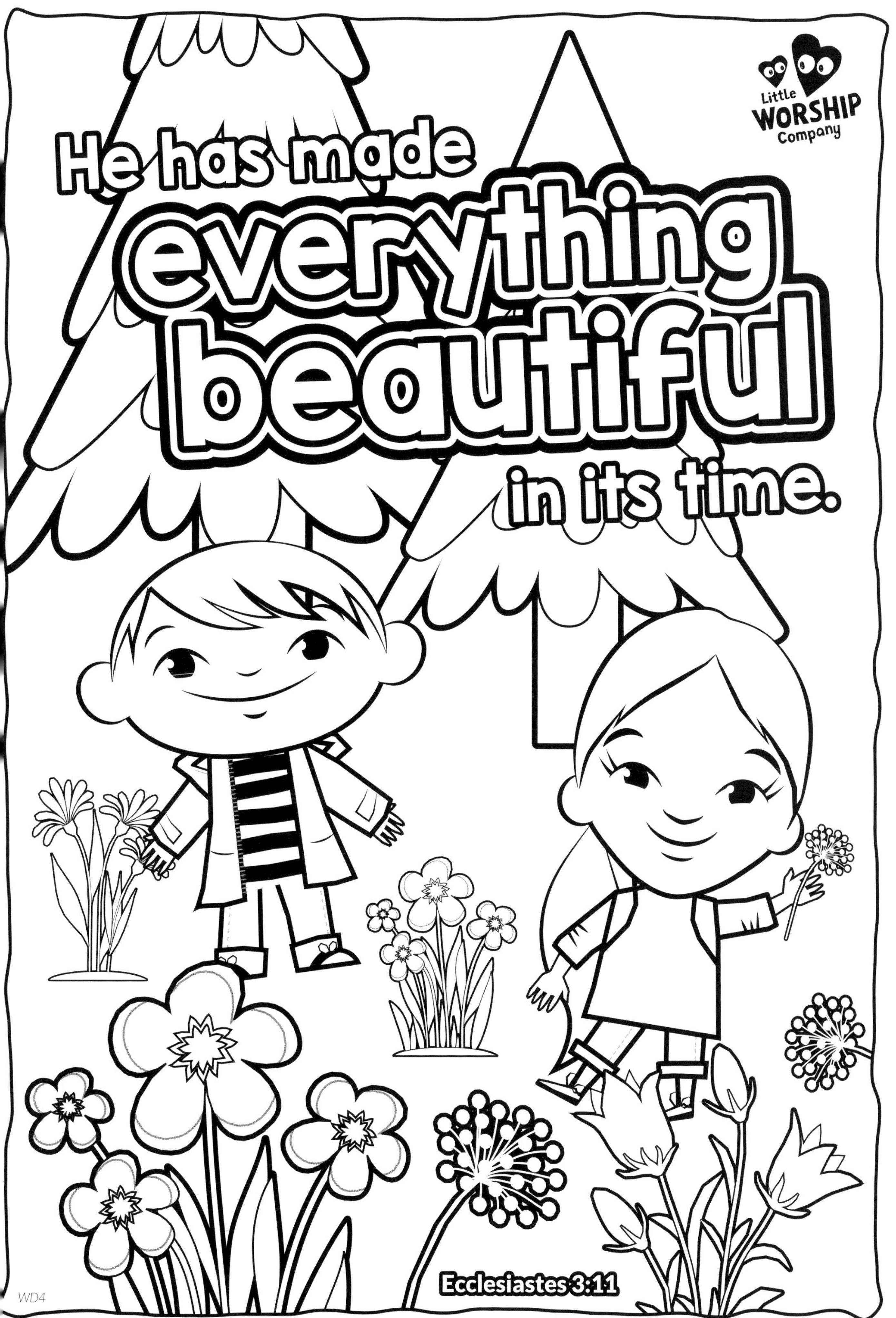
Little WORSHIP Company
He has made
everything
beautiful
in its time.
Ecclesiastes 3:11
WD4

5 God gives me all I need today

In this session, the children will:

- explore the miracle of Jesus' feeding of the 5,000
- reflect on God's promise to provide whatever we need

2 Corinthians 9:8 (LWC)

God is able to give you all you need - and more!

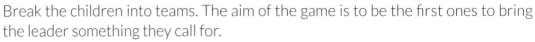

ICE-BREAKER

Preparation level

GAME: "BRING ME..."

Break the children into teams. The aim of the game is to be the first ones to bring the leader something they call for.

For example:

"Bring me..."

- two shoes joined together
- something red
- three socks inside out
- a watch
- something I can eat

Tip: When playing the game, it is best to nominate one person from the group to bring the items to avoid too much chaos!

LITTLE BIG QUESTION

If you could ask for one thing right now, what would it be?

LITTLE BIG IDEA

ILLUSTRATION: 5,000 HUNGRY PEOPLE

You will need: *the* ***5,000 Hungry People*** *sheet, found in the appendix*

Explore Jesus' miracle of the feeding of the 5,000, found in Matthew 14:13-21.

To make the story interactive, read the **Little Worship Company** version found in the appendix.

You might like to show the session *God is amazing* from the DVD. 

MESSAGE

- Ask the children: have you ever really, really needed something? You might share a story about a time when you have needed something.
- There are all sorts of things that we need every day. Sometimes these are things we can see and touch – like food to eat and clothes to wear. Sometimes we need things that we can't see, but they're just as important. We might need courage to do something difficult. Or we might need a friend to talk to.
- 2 Corinthians 9:8 says, "God is able to give you all you need – and more!" In other words, God has absolutely everything we could ever need each day and more besides.
- He also loves to give things to His children. Jesus said that we should ask God for our 'daily bread', which is His way of describing all the things we need each day. In our story, Jesus proved how God was able to give them actual bread by feeding 5,000 very hungry people!
- This is a special promise for us too. If you need anything today, or if there's something you're worried about, you can talk to God about it. Ask Him to give you what you need – you'll be amazed at what He will do!

LET'S WORSHIP

DVD

Song: *Great is Thy Faithfulness*

Singalong: *Prayer Song*

Prayer: Wonderful Day thank you prayer

LITTLE GROUPS

DAILY BREAD 

You will need: *dough, greaseproof baking paper, access to an oven, plates, butter/jam, etc.*

Preparation: Make some dough before the session. See **Get Crafty!** for the recipe.

Invite the children to model their dough to make some interestingly-shaped rolls. As you make the rolls together, talk with the children about anything they might want to ask God for today.

Put them on greaseproof paper, remembering to write the children's names on the paper. Bake the bread rolls for 10-15 minutes in a preheated oven (220°C). Eat together or take them home.

SESSION PRAYER

Dear God, thank you that You care for us so much. Thank you that You promise to give us everything that we need, today and every day. **Amen.**

GET CRAFTY!

Difficulty level
suitable for all ages · for older children

Continue exploring the theme of God's provision with these crafts.

1 FRUIT KEBABS AND CHOCOLATE SAUCE

You will need: *soft fruits that can be easily chopped with a plastic/blunt knife, child-friendly knife, chopping board, wooden skewers, plates*

To make the fruit kebabs:

- Choose some soft fruits.
- Cut them into chunks.
- Carefully push a wooden skewer through the middle of each piece of fruit.
- Repeat until the skewer is full up.

Tip: You might like to eat these in the session. Why not serve them with a little dish of warm chocolate sauce?

2 RAINBOW PIZZA

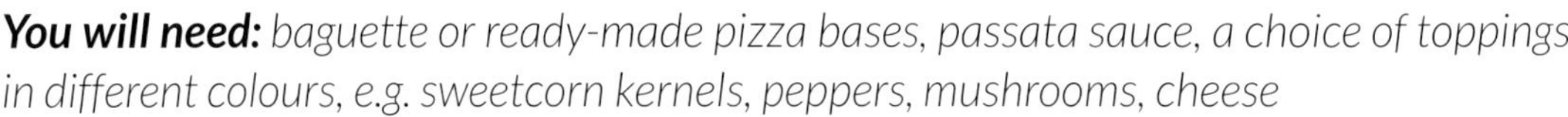

You will need: *baguette or ready-made pizza bases, passata sauce, a choice of toppings in different colours, e.g. sweetcorn kernels, peppers, mushrooms, cheese*

To make the pizza:

- Cover a pizza base or baguette slice in passata.
- Add different toppings of your choice.
- Bake the pizza in a moderately hot oven for 10-15 minutes.

3 DAILY BREAD

Help the children to remember God's promise to provide our daily bread by baking some delicious rolls.

Tip: The dough will need one hour to rise. You may like to make the dough in advance and then invite the children to make shaped rolls, baking and eating them in the session.

Recipe:

- 500g strong white flour
- 7g sachet of yeast
- Pinch of salt
- 3 tbsp vegetable oil
- 300ml water

To make the dough:

- Mix the flour, yeast and salt in a bowl.
- Make a well in the middle. Pour in the water and oil and mix it up.
- Tip onto a floured surface and knead for 5-10 minutes.
- Leave to rise for one hour until doubled in size.

To make the rolls:

- Divide the dough into small pieces. Mould into interesting shapes.
- Put onto a covered baking tray and bake in a hot oven for 10-15 minutes.
- When cooked, place on a wire rack to cool.

WD5
God is able to give you all you need – and more!
What has God given you?
Little WORSHIP Company
2 Corinthians 9:8 LWC

6 God gives me a fresh start today

In this session, the children will:

- reflect on some of the bad choices we might make in the day
- understand that even if we make mistakes, God loves us and gives us another chance

1 John 1:9 (LWC)

If we say sorry to God when we get something wrong, we can be sure that He will always, always make it right again.

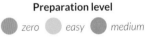

Preparation level

zero easy medium

ICE-BREAKER

GAME: BEANBAG THROW

You will need: *beanbags, 3 buckets per team*

Break the children into teams and get them to line up, one behind the other behind a line. Place 3 buckets at a short distance away: the first about 2 metres away from the line; the next about 4 metres; the last about 6 metres away. Give the team members a beanbag each.

The aim of the game is to get all the team's beanbags into the first bucket (i.e. the one that's 2 metres away). The team takes it in turns to throw. When the challenge has been completed, they collect the beanbags and repeat the process for the next bucket (i.e. the one that's 4 metres away). It should be harder – more beanbags will miss the target. When this happens, a leader should collect the beanbag and give it to the next person in the line without a beanbag. When all the beanbags make it in, the team repeats the process – this time aiming for the last bucket.

You may like to refer to the game later in the session – that we often 'miss the target' and get things wrong in the course of the day. But the good news is, God always gives us another go.

LITTLE BIG QUESTION

What's the messiest you have ever been?

LITTLE BIG IDEA

ILLUSTRATION: WHAT A MESS!

You will need: *a whiteboard easel, dry wipe markers, a cloth, a still life object*

Talk about how much you love drawing. Bring out something to draw – for example, a fruit bowl. Begin drawing on the whiteboard. Make sure that the children can see your board as you draw.

Make lots of mistakes along the way, but don't rub anything out. Deliberately make it look messy.

At the end, look at the mess you have made of your drawing. What can you do? Perhaps you could rub it out and try again?

LINK TO MESSAGE

Despite our best intentions, things don't always turn out as we hope they will. We make lots of mistakes along the way. And the same is often true of our daily life.

MESSAGE

- Ask the children: Have you ever said something that made somebody a bit sad? Or have you ever done something you wish you hadn't? (Don't ask what – just get a show of hands!)
- God wants us to live each day in a way that will make Him and other people happy. He wants us to be kind to the people around us and to help them.
- But we don't always do it. In fact, we often end up doing the opposite. Sometimes during the day we say unkind or cross things and make people sad. Sometimes we say things that aren't true. Sometimes we do mean things.
- When this happens, it can leave us feeling unhappy and sad that we messed up. But there is good news, because God promises to give us another chance.
- 1 John 1:9 says, "If we say sorry to God when we get something wrong, we can be sure that He will always, always make it right again." God knows all about the mistakes we make – nothing surprises Him! He also sees our heart and knows when we are sorry for the bad choices we make.
- There's nothing we can do that stops God from loving us. No matter what kind of mess we might make in the day, God will always forgive us. When we say sorry to Him, He lets us begin again – just like it never happened.

LET'S WORSHIP

Song: *How Deep the Father's Love*

Singalong: *Prayer Song*

Prayer: Wonderful Day thank you prayer

LITTLE GROUPS

HANDPRINT PRAYERS

You will need: *paint, roll of paper, washing-up bowls, towels*

In groups, reflect on some of the things we might do that hurt God and others.

Put out a long roll of paper. One by one, invite the children to cover the side of their hand in paint and print it twice on the paper – vertically and horizontally – to make a cross.

Invite them to wash their messy hands in the water, remembering that Jesus took our mess and mistakes so that we could have clean hearts before God.

Close with the **session prayer.**

SESSION PRAYER

Dear God, thank you that whatever we do, You still love us. We're sorry for the times when we make a mess and hurt other people. Thank you that You promise to give us a second chance, today and every day. **Amen.**

GET CRAFTY!

Difficulty level

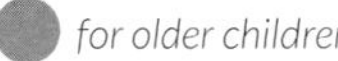

Use these crafts to explore the theme of forgiveness.

1 WATER PLAY

Set up a sensory area using water. Fill up a big, deep tray with water. Include various pots, pans, cups and utensils with holes to run the water though.

Use it to reflect on how there's nothing too messy for God to clean up.

2 BOTTLE SHAKERS

You will need: *empty washing-up bottles, rice grains, decorating materials*

To make the shaker:

- Pour some dry rice into an empty bottle and screw the lid back on.
- Decorate the bottle to finish.

Use the shakers in worship, remembering that God makes our hearts clean!

3 KITE

You will need: *a large piece of paper, decorating materials, ribbons, scissors, sticky tape*

Each child will need a large piece of paper.

To make the kite:

- Draw a line from the middle of the top of the paper to the edges of both sides, then down again into the middle of the bottom.
- Cut out the kite shape. Decorate it with tissue paper, paints or even colouring pens.
- Attach a long ribbon to the back of the kite with tape.
- Add a few more ribbons to make an interesting tail.

You might like to draw a large cross connecting the corners of the kite. Use the kite to remember that because Jesus died, we can know forgiveness and freedom.

WD6
He will
always, always
make it right again!
1 John 1:9 LWC
Little WORSHIP Company

7 God holds me in His hands today

In this session, the children will:

- explore the story of Jesus calming the storm
- understand that God is bigger than anything that worries us, and that He promises us His peace

Psalm 46:10

Be still and know that I am God.

Tip: As this session explores the story of Jesus and His disciples out on the Sea of Galilee, you may like to imagine that your hall/room is one large boat that the children board at the beginning.

ICE-BREAKER

Preparation level

zero *easy* *medium*

GAME: ALL ABOARD! 

You will need space to play this game.

Before you play the game, explain the different actions that accompany the following commands.

- **Bow** – run to the front of the room
- **Stern** – run to the back of the room
- **Port** – run to the left-hand side of the room
- **Starboard** – run to the right-hand side of the room
- **Scrub the decks** – drop to the floor and scrub
- **Climb the rigging** – mime climbing
- **Captain's coming** – stand and salute
- **Lifeboats** – find a partner, sit down facing each other and row
- **Shark attack** – run around pretending to be a shark

To play the game, the leader calls out commands which the children need to follow. Either run this as a warm-up, or play to win, with the last person to follow the command declared 'out'.

LITTLE BIG QUESTION

Who is the first person you talk to when you need help?

LITTLE BIG IDEA

ILLUSTRATION: STILL THROUGH THE STORM

You will need: *the* ***Still Through the Storm*** *sheet, found in the appendix, assorted props as suggested in the appendix*

Board your 'boat' and explore Jesus' miracle of the calming of the storm, found in Mark 4:35-41.

To make the story interactive, read the **Little Worship Company** version found in the appendix.

You might like to show the **session Bible verse**, found on the DVD, here. 

MESSAGE

- Ask the children if they have ever heard the word 'worry'. Can they explain what it is? What kinds of things might worry us?
- We have been thinking about God's amazing promises to us and what they mean for us each day. One of the wonderful things the Bible tells us is that we don't need to feel worried or afraid, because God loves us and is with us.
- In our Bible story, the disciples felt worried and scared. They were in the middle of a big storm, out on the wild sea. But although it seemed frightening, Jesus was with them. He was stronger than the storm. As long as the disciples were with Jesus, they were completely safe.
- Psalm 46:10 says, "Be still and know that I am God." It means that we can feel completely calm because God is amazing and powerful. He's bigger than anything in this world and there's nothing He can't do.
- What's more, He really, really loves us. Even if we face something a bit scary, which we're worried about, we know that God is beside us. And when we talk to Him about it, He helps us and gives His special peace.

LET'S WORSHIP

Song: *Hope Song*

Singalong: *Prayer Song*

Prayer: Wonderful Day thank you prayer

LITTLE GROUPS

THROUGH THE STORM

In groups, reflect on the Bible story. Ask the children to imagine that they were a disciple in the boat.

- How would they feel at the beginning of the storm?
- What would they want to say to Jesus then?
- How would they feel when Jesus calmed the storm?
- What would they want to say to Jesus then?

Ask the children if they would like to pray about any situations – for themselves or someone they know. Close with the **session prayer.**

SESSION PRAYER

Dear God, thank you that You are bigger than everything in this world. Thank you that we don't need to worry about anything, because You're in charge – today and every day. **Amen.**

GET CRAFTY!

Difficulty level

Use these crafts to remind the children that we never need to worry, because God is with us and looks after us.

1 APPLE SAILING BOATS

You will need: *apples cut in half, craft (lollipop) sticks, card, decorating materials, scissors, glue*

Use this craft to introduce or reflect on the story of Jesus calming the storm.

To make an apple sailing boat:

- Cut out a card triangle flag and glue it to the top of the stick.
- Decorate a small rectangle of card to make the sail.
- Make a small slit in the top middle and bottom middle of the card sail. Thread the stick through.
- Using your half apple, push the stick sail into the sliced part of the apple.
- Sail the boat in the sink, in the bath, or even on a pond or lake!

2 ANCHORS

You will need: *a large sheet of card, scissors, decorating materials*

Preparation: Create a 'half an anchor' template for the children to use.

To make the anchor:

- Fold a large sheet of card in half and draw around the template.
- Cut it out and unfold the card to make an anchor shape.
- Decorate the anchor. (You might want to include the Bible verse.)

As you make the craft, reflect on how anchors keep boats still and safe, even in stormy weather. Likewise, we can be still, knowing that God is big enough and loving enough to keep us safe, even in difficult times.

3 NIGHT LIGHTS

You will need: *a jam jar, craft glue, tissue paper squares, ribbon, an LED candle*

To make your night light:

- Cover a jam jar with craft glue.
- Layer on colourful pieces of tissue paper.
- After you have covered the jar, add another layer of glue.
- When dry, decorate with a ribbon.
- Put an LED candle in the base of the jar to complete your night light.

As you make the craft, you might talk about how the children feel about the dark, and the difference a light makes. Talk about how God is like light in the darkness.

WD7
Be still
and know that
I am God.
Psalm 46:10
Little
WORSHIP
Company

8 God is with me today, tomorrow and always

In this session, the children will:

- reflect on the promise that God is always with them, even as they sleep

Proverbs 3:24 (LWC)

When you go to bed, you will not be scared. When you lie down, your sleep will be sweet.

Tip: This session is themed around 'bedtime'. You might want to set the hall/room up to reflect the theme – dimmed lighting, cushions and blankets around, a 'bedtime story' corner, etc.

ICE-BREAKER

Preparation level: zero, easy, medium

GAME: BEDTIME!

You will need: *some dressing gowns, some bowls of water, towels, beakers, a jug of water, some simple picture books*

This is a bedtime-themed obstacle relay race.

Break the children into teams. To play the game, each team member must complete a number of bedtime-themed challenges one after the other:

- Put on the dressing gown (for the duration of the challenges).
- Wash and dry your face at the bowl.
- Have a bedtime drink (i.e. drink water from a beaker). Note: a team member will need to refill the water in between challenges.
- 'Read' a bedtime story aloud (just read the first page of the picture book).

When the team member has completed these challenges, they run back to their team and pass the dressing gown to the next team member, who then completes the challenges. The first team to have all their members complete the challenges wins.

Tip: If space or numbers are an issue, you could play a round of 'Sleeping Lions' instead. All the children must lie still on the floor without moving, speaking or laughing.

LITTLE BIG QUESTION

What's the best dream you ever had?

LITTLE BIG IDEA

ILLUSTRATION: THE GOD OF BEDTIME

With younger children, role play bedtime with a teddy.

You will need: *a teddy or soft toy, a bag, a flannel, a small bath toy, a toothbrush, a reading book, a doll's crib, blankets*

Introduce your teddy to the children. Explain that teddy has had a busy day and that it's time for him to go to bed.

Ask the children about the different elements of their bedtime routine. Bring out items from your bag to role play those parts of the routine with teddy. You could include:

- bath time
- brushing teeth
- putting pyjamas on
- reading a story

Tuck teddy into bed. Look a bit surprised. Explain that teddy says that he doesn't want to go to bed. It seems that teddy is a bit scared! He doesn't like it when it's dark. He feels alone.

Use this as a way into sharing the message that God is with us (below).

With older children, share these verses from Psalm 121.

"He won't let you stumble, your Guardian God won't fall asleep. Not on your life! Israel's Guardian will never doze or sleep." (Psalm 121:3-4, MSG)

You will need: *large paper, marker pens*

Run this like a game of 'Hangman' where the letters of each word are missing, represented by dashes. The children take turns guessing a letter, which the leader then fills in. If the children guess a letter which doesn't feature in the Bible verse, the leader draws part of a picture. Aim for a simple picture of a stick man lying in a bed. Can the children work out the Bible verse before 'Sticky' goes to sleep?

Tip: With larger numbers of children, play the game in teams, with each team choosing a letter between them.

You might like to show the **session Bible verse**, found on the DVD, here. 

MESSAGE

- Over the last few weeks, we have been looking at some of God's amazing promises to us.
- We've thought about how each day is God's day. We've explored the things He gives us every day: good things to enjoy; anything we need; forgiveness when we mess up; and peace when we feel scared.
- But God's promises aren't just for the daytime. The Bible promises that God is still with us even as we're lying in our beds.
- Proverbs 3:24 says, "When you go to bed, you will not be scared. When you lie down, your sleep will be sweet." It means that we don't need to worry at any time. God doesn't clock off or go to sleep. Instead, He watches over us day and night. If we ever wake up worrying, or feeling frightened, He's with us and He promises to give us His peace.
- God is always with us. Day or night, He's there. At home or away on holiday, He's there. And He loves us so much. We never need to worry, because God is with us today, tonight, tomorrow and always – our Heavenly Dad and our best friend.

LET'S WORSHIP

DVD

Song: *Be Still*

Singalong: *Prayer Song*

Prayer: Wonderful Day thank you prayer

LITTLE GROUPS

HOT CHOCOLATE

You will need: *mugs, ready-made hot chocolate, whipped cream, marshmallows, sprinkles, biscuits*

In groups, make some luxurious hot chocolate drinks. As you drink them together, reflect on the promise that God is with us everywhere, all the time. You might want to ask:

- Where is the furthest you have ever been? (God is there!)
- Are there any times of the day or places you go where you feel worried? (God is there!)

Tip: You might want to add to the 'bedtime' feel by providing sleeping bags or blankets for the children to sit in while they have their hot chocolate.

SESSION PRAYER

Dear God, thank you that we never need to be afraid because You love us SO much. Thank you that You promise to watch over us today, tonight, tomorrow, and every day. **Amen.**

GET CRAFTY!

Difficulty level

suitable for all ages *for older children*

Use these bedtime-themed crafts to remind the children that God watches over them all the time, even as they sleep.

PATCHWORK BED 

You will need: *A4 card, coloured paper squares, glue, cut-out people, pens*

Preparation: Cut the A4 pieces of card in half, lengthways, to make strips of card.

Each child will need a strip of card.

To make your bed:

- Bring the bottom of your card up to about 3cm from the top, and fold. (There needs to be enough space left for a 'pillow'.)
- Put glue along the vertical edges and stick the halves of card together. (**Note:** leave the horizontal edge open.)
- To make a patchwork-effect blanket, stick different pieces of coloured paper over the folded card.
- Draw a rectangle at the top of the card to make your pillow.
- Decorate the cut-out person, and put it into bed for a good night's sleep.

As you make the beds, reflect on how God is with us even as we go to sleep.

2 BEDTIME BISCUITS

Preparation: Depending on your situation, you might like to make the dough using the recipe below ahead of the session.

With the children, cut the biscuits into 'night-time' shapes – e.g. moon and stars – and decorate them with white icing, sprinkles, and silver balls. If running this activity with younger children, you might want to bake them in advance too, leaving them just to decorate them.

Recipe:

- 100g butter
- 100g sugar
- 1 egg
- 275g plain flour
- 400g icing sugar
- 3 tbsp water
- Decorations – silver balls, sprinkles, etc.

To make the biscuits:

- Mix the butter and sugar.
- Beat in 1 egg.
- Fold in the flour.
- Slowly mix until it is a firm dough.
- Roll out the dough and cut into shapes.
- Bake in a moderate oven for 12 minutes.

To make the icing:

- Sift the icing sugar into a bowl and add a few tablespoons of water, until it makes a paste.

3 DVD 'SLEEP WELL' SIGN

You will need: *a blank door sign (available to buy, or make your own), toy cars, paint, pens or letter stickers, additional decorating materials*

Each child will need a blank door sign.

To make the sign:

- Dip the wheels of a toy car in paint, and drive the car over one side of the sign.
- Wait a moment for it to dry. Attach foam lettering or write on it with a thick pen the phrase 'Shhh! I'm sleeping!'
- Repeat on the other side, this time using the phrase 'Yes! I'm awake!'
- Decorate the sign with extra craft materials.

Remind the children that as they put their bedtime sign on the door, they can be sure that God is still with them.

WD8
When you lie down,
your sleep will be sweet.
Little
WORSHIP
Company
Proverbs 3:24 LWC

WONDERFUL DAY
All-age worship

At the end of the curriculum course, you may like to lead a Sunday morning, all-age worship service on the curriculum's theme, inviting the children to participate in leading it.

Follow or adapt the service plan below as appropriate for your congregation.

WELCOME

Welcome the congregation to the service.

OPENING PRAYER

Dear God, [this morning] we declare that today is Your day. We want to celebrate You today. We want to worship You today. We want to meet with You today.

As we come together now, we pray that You will open our eyes to see You more and our hearts to love You more today. **Amen.**

WORSHIP

Sing a couple of **songs** from the **Wonderful Day** DVD.

Say this **child-friendly prayer** together.

ALL-AGE LITURGY

Thank you, God, for this wonderful day!

Thank you for fun times.

Thank you for friends to play with.

Thank you for laughing.

Thank you for the people who look after us.

Thank you for playing.

Thank you for family.

Thank you for food to eat.

Thank you for cosy beds.

Thank you for the dreams You give us.

Amen.

CHILDREN'S SLOT

Invite the children to the front to talk about the different things they have learnt over the last few weeks. They might like to share some of the crafts they have made, or any memory verses they have learnt.

The children may also like to sing a **Wonderful Day singalong song.** Perhaps they could teach it to the adults!

WORD

Read one or more of the suggested **Bible readings** (or choose your own). Invite a range of readers – young and old – to do this.

- **Philippians 4:4-7** A tremendous promise that God is always with us, giving us His peace.
- **Psalm 46** A celebration of the God who holds everything in His hands – including us.
- **Matthew 6:9-14** The Lord's Prayer – a reminder of the great God who promises to meet our needs daily, who forgives us and who protects us.

MESSAGE

Share the suggested message below or create your own.

Key Bible passage: Philippians 4:4-7

Key message: As we spend our days in prayer and praise, we can know God's peace.

Preparation: Have a big board at the ready, with the following formula (with blanks) written up:

P_________ + P_________ = P_________

INTRODUCTION

- Invite the congregation to share their idea of a 'wonderful day'. What would it entail?
- Explain that you have discovered a secret formula to ensure that **every day** is a wonderful day – and it's something you found in Philippians 4. *[Reveal the board and fill in the blanks as you lead through the reflection.]*

REFLECTION

- Over the last few weeks the children have been exploring the idea of a **Wonderful Day.** Psalm 118:24 (LWC) says:
  "This is the day that the Lord has made. Let us rejoice and be glad in it."
- Each day is a wonderful gift from God – and one that we can share with Him and know Him in. But how?
- The first P is **praise.** Paul says that we should "rejoice in the Lord always" (verse 4) and be thankful (verse 6). Every day there are things we can praise God for: the sunshine, food, our families, and much more. We can also praise God for Jesus – that because of Jesus' death and resurrection, we will always be God's friend. As we learn to praise God for these everyday things, we become more aware of God's goodness to us and presence with us.
- The second P is **prayer.** Some days it's easy to rejoice because they're so much fun! But other days, we might feel a little overwhelmed or troubled. Paul writes that we don't need to worry about anything – we just need to talk to God about it. We can ask Him for the things we need. We can share the things which are on our mind with Him. God is always listening.
- When we put **praise** and **prayer** together, we get something rather special: God's **peace.** Paul writes that "the peace of God, which transcends all understanding, will guard [our] hearts and... minds" (verse 7). We don't

always know how the day will turn out – whether it will be the best day ever or one we would rather forget! But the Bible promises that God walks beside us in all of it. As we daily thank Him for His goodness and share with Him our concerns, every day will be wonderful – because we will know how much we are loved by Him.

PRAYERS

RAYS OF SUNSHINE

Use this activity as a way of praising God for His faithfulness each day.

You will need: *a big, yellow circle (the sun), strips of yellow paper (the sun's rays), pens, sticky tack*

Preparation: In the big, yellow circle, write Psalm 118:24:
"This is the day that the Lord has made. Let us rejoice and be glad in it."

- Reflect on the words of Psalm 118:24. God is in every day. And we can celebrate all the good things He gives to us and does for us each day.
- Give out the yellow strips. Invite the congregation to talk about the things that they are especially thankful for today. Ask them to write down or draw some of these on the strips of paper.
- Invite them to bring them to the front and stick them around the yellow circle to create a 'sun' picture.
- At the end, close in a general prayer of thanksgiving and praise.

FAMILY EUCHARIST

You will need: *bread, non-alcoholic red juice*

Jesus taught us to ask God for our daily bread. It was His way of describing everything we need. His words took on new meaning in the light of the Last Supper, when the bread came to signify His body. God promises to provide our material needs each day; and in Jesus, we can be sure that God's unconditional love, forgiveness and grace are ours too.

With this in mind – and if your church tradition allows it – you might like to take the opportunity to share the Lord's Supper with the whole church family.

WORSHIP

Sing one or two songs from the **Wonderful Day** DVD. (You may like to take up an offering here and/or say the Lord's Prayer together.)

BLESSING AND DISMISSAL

Formally close the service.

CLOSING BLESSING

May we see more of God's goodness to us. May we feel more of God's presence with us. And may we know more of God's love for us – today, tomorrow and every day. **Amen.**

Wonderful Day: Session 1: God's day worksheet

Today is God's day!

Every day is a special day from God!
Take 5 minutes every day this week and ask yourself...

Where did I SEE God today? For example – is there anything you're thankful for? Did somebody help you? Did you feel peaceful or brave when you had to do something difficult?

When did I SERVE God today? For example – when you were helpful to others, or said something kind, or gave something away.

	Today, I **saw** God when...	Today, I **served** God when...
Sunday		
Monday		
Tuesday		
Wednesday		
Thursday		
Friday		
Saturday		

WHAT A SURPRISE!

Each day is full of surprises. Select some everyday scenarios from the list below that are appropriate for your children. As you read them out, invite the children to share how that 'surprise' would leave them feeling.

For younger children, keep the response very simple. Invite the children either to pull a face showing some basic emotions – e.g. happy or sad – or to put their thumbs up, down or somewhere in the middle to indicate a positive, negative or 'unsure' response. You might ask them to reflect on their feelings – why would this event make them feel this way?

For older children, you might ask them to differentiate between more complex emotions. For example – would this surprise make you feel happy, excited, sad or anxious?

- Your dad makes you pancakes for breakfast.
- You are given a surprise spelling test at school.
- Someone takes your favourite toy away from you in the playground.
- It's sunny, so you go to the park for a really long time.
- Someone says something mean to you.
- You are given a certificate at school.
- You stop off for sweets at the corner shop.
- You go swimming.
- You fall off your bike/fall over in the garden.
- You find out that your grandparent has had to go into hospital.

5,000 HUNGRY PEOPLE

BASED ON MATTHEW 14:13-21

This is a version of Jesus' feeding of the five thousand. Read the text below and invite the children to join in with counting out the different numbers featured in the story.

You may also like to have some props or pictures to help the story come alive – for example, some real bread to pass around at the appropriate point.

THE STORY

Jesus was tired. He'd been travelling and teaching and needed a rest. So He headed out to a quiet place with His twelve disciples.

Count them with me: 1, 2, 3, 4, 5, 6, 7, 8, 9, 10, 11, 12.

But the crowds found out where Jesus was. They wanted to see Him, so they followed Him there – five thousand of them!

Count them with me: 1 thousand, 2 thousand, 3 thousand, 4 thousand, 5 thousand.

Jesus spent the afternoon with the crowds, teaching them about God and healing anyone who was sick. The hours flew past and before long it was seven o'clock.

Count the hours with me: 1 o'clock, 2 o'clock, 3 o'clock, 4 o'clock, 5 o'clock, 6 o'clock, 7 o'clock.

Everybody was beginning to feel hungry. The disciples went to Jesus and told Him to send the crowds away to get food. But Jesus told them to find everyone some food. The disciples were confused. All they had were five loaves and two fish.

Count them with me: 1, 2, 3, 4, 5 loaves and 1, 2 fish.

Jesus took the five loaves. He took the two fish. With two hands held high to heaven, He thanked God and broke the bread.

And then He gave it to His disciples, who gave it to the people. Everybody ate their fill – and in the end there were twelve basketfuls left over.

Count them with me: 1, 2, 3, 4, 5, 6, 7, 8, 9, 10, 11, 12.

REFLECTION

Jesus performed an amazing miracle that day.

Imagine that you had been there. How would you have felt after you'd had your meal?